16.95 ✓

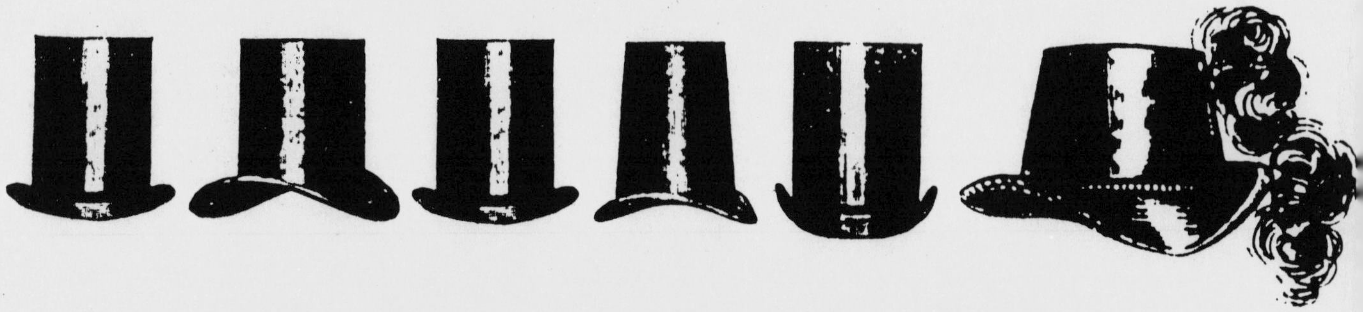

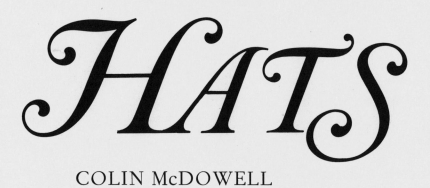

HATS

STATUS, STYLE
AND GLAMOUR

with over 300 illustrations,
82 in colour

COLIN McDOWELL

THAMES AND HUDSON

For Marina Sturdza

Picture Research: Georgina Bruckner

Text © 1992 Colin McDowell
Layout © 1992 Thames and Hudson Ltd, London

First paperback edition 1997

British Library Cataloguing-in-Publication Data
A catalogue record for this book is available from the British Library
ISBN 0-500-27944-6

Printed and bound in Singapore by C.S. Graphics Pte Ltd

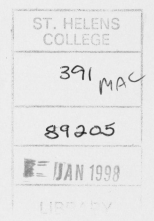

CONTENTS

*A*ll the basic hat shapes were created very early in the history of mankind. Over the last five hundred years the development of headwear has been more a process of changing scale, proportion and decoration than of changing style. In fact, there are only two styles: brimmed and unbrimmed. And there are only two basic forms: caps and hats. The history of modern headwear is concerned with variations on these. We can go further and say that for most of the time there have been only two materials: felt and straw. But it would be wrong to imagine that such limitations make the subject of hats narrow or predictable. On the contrary, headwear has been used to show pride, humour, resourcefulness and imagination with a variety that few other items of clothing can emulate and none can surpass. Over the centuries the hat has been pre-eminently the item of dress that could best proclaim – quickly, effectively and dramatically – the personality and status of the wearer.

As was true of most subsequent hats, the very earliest example, the pileus, combined status with practicality. In this case, however, the status was invested not in materials, trimming and scale, as has been the case with modern hats, but in the fact that only certain classes were permitted to wear it. The pileus was nothing more elaborate than a skullcap, made of leather, linen or wool, that enveloped the head and stopped at ear level. From it developed the petasus, which was little more than the pileus with a brim. Add the cowl or hood, the turban and the crown, and, in essence, we have the styles that are the basis of all the headwear created since the Graeco-Roman period. During the Middle Ages, the development of the hat was a slow process as, indeed, was all fashion change. Most men wore hats only when travelling; women followed the tradition of Greek and Roman matrons and covered their heads with scarves or the hoods of cloaks.

In the eleventh century, the most popular style for European men was the leather bonnet. Tightly fitting and secured under the chin by ribbons, it resembled a modern baby's bonnet. It was condemned across Europe as effeminate by nations where, for generations, the nobleman had proclaimed his superiority over the serf by wearing his hair long, luxuriant and rarely covered. Now, despite the furore, led by the Emperor Otto the Great, the bonnet – more frequently worn without ties – became the distinguishing sign of the noble. Further, it became a fashion object and by the beginning of the fourteenth century magnificent versions in velvet, brocade and silk, ornamented with plumes, feathers and jewels, had appeared.

By this time the hood had also developed into a sophisticated and stylish item, not easily distinguished from a hat, and worn like a cap with its long ends frequently wrapped around the head to make a turban. Whereas in the early Middle Ages hats had been worn only occasionally, now that they were fashionable they were worn almost universally, indoors as well as outdoors. Guests at banquets, bankers in their halls, merchants in their shops and artisans in their workrooms all wore coverings on the head. Hats had become an important part of the gorgeousness of display that characterized Europe as the Middle Ages drew to a close.

It was a period when men of power, confident in their superiority over women and peasants, felt themselves beyond criticism, and allowed their dress to become overtly sexual. Their headwear in particular took on a saucy salaciousness, somewhat similar to that of the pointed poulaine found on the feet of every man of fashion. The hood that had been universally worn by men throughout Europe for over a century became elongated at the back and began to dangle like an animal's tail. Originally a court fashion, this style, called the liripipe, eventually swept across all classes. Often padded, it had all the sexual suggestiveness of a snake. In fact, it was a clearly proclaimed phallic symbol and was worn and manipulated by men who were fully aware of its power of suggestion. Although not the most practical item of clothing, the liripipe gave a confidence to the man of fashion that was not lightly tossed aside. In fact, so reluctant was he to abandon the style that when modish dress moved on and reinstated the smaller, practical cap for normal, easeful wear, he wore the cap and liripipe together – one for practical reasons and the other entirely for show.

Then, as now, women were no more immune to the idiocies of fashion than were their menfolk. The fifteenth-century hennin, for example, was surely one of the

The 15-century hennin. *The Hours of Mary of Burgundy*, illuminated manuscript, *c.* 1477.

most bizarre and impractical items of dress ever created. But, like most female styles, it was merely an attempt to keep up with and even outdo the galloping megalomania apparent in men's styles and can be seen simply as an exaggeration of the tall tapering crowns that were a popular male fashion.

Just how high the hennin soared is a matter of doubt. No examples have survived and we are left to draw conclusions from the records left by artists and sculptors. It is important to remember that works of art — even portraits — are products of the imagination and just as modern fashion artists exaggerate scale and elongate proportions, it might well be that the high hennins that have come down to us in paintings are dramatizations of headwear which, in reality, was much more prosaic in scale.

Regardless of scale, the hennin and its progeny, the butterfly headdress, which between them dominated the fifteenth century, conformed to the chief rules of women's fashion until the twentieth century. They were inconvenient, impractical and incommoding. Worn with the long gown that women trailed through the later Middle Ages, the hennin highlighted the two major facts of life for a noblewoman. She was seen as an object of beauty by her men — a graceful, elongated moving statue — but, more sinisterly, she was forced by her dress, from the unstable hennin to the ermine-bound hemline, to be an utterly impractical object, incapable of work and requiring the assistance of servants for even quite minor physical exertions. It is within these terms that the hennin must be considered. It shackled as much as it glorified. When, following the male move towards the flat low bonnet that came in at the beginning of the sixteenth century, the steeple headgear disappeared and women began to wear the hood, this change coincided with an increase in the width of shoulders and skirts, which severely restricted mobility, so that a freedom gained in one part of the body was lost in another.

In all of this exaggeration, the gaudy appeal of the crown was not forgotten. Since status fashion is about proclaiming the power of the wearer's wealth and social position, it follows that the wealthiest and most socially superior being is the one who wears a crown. Thus, though it obviously could not become a fashion item, the crown was the object all other headwear fashions were emulating. That is why hats for both men and women at this time set out to imitate the crown's magnificence. Ornamented with jewels, semi-precious stones and pearls, they were an obvious sign of the wearer's wealth and position. As bonnets and toques became more architectural in shape and less easy to decorate, the hatband was frequently used to display status. Studded with jewels and finely embroidered with pearls, it proclaimed the gentleman as surely as did his swaggering walk and careless indifference to his fellows.

Even Cromwell, Lord Protector of England, wore a hat with a carcanet of diamonds as a buckle and, legend has it, such uncharacteristic show paid off; the buckle twice saved his life. At Worcester, a Royalist fired his blunderbuss point blank at Cromwell's head and once, when Cromwell was travelling to the Guildhall to dine with the Lord Mayor and the sheriffs, a woman wishing to avenge the execution of Lord Francis Villiers aimed at Cromwell from an upstairs window in Ludgate. On both occasions, the buckle deflected the shot.

Costly jewellery was not the only way in which the controlling classes awarded themselves magnificence. From the fourteenth to the seventeenth century, men of rank also enjoyed wearing feathers, which were expensive and rare and therefore a

The jewelled and feathered hat of the 16th century. Portrait of George Clifford, 3rd Earl of Cumberland, by Nicholas Hilliard (c. 1547–1619).

distinctive symbol of rank and riches. The broad-brimmed feathered hat was particularly popular but, for the majority, headwear was much more prosaic. For everyday wear the cap was most usual. Each class and every profession developed its own type of headwear: the plain, flat bonnet of the scholar; the high bonnet of the physician, the townsmen in their black caps and the members of the old-established families in jewelled caps. Only the peasants were left out in the cold. The bonnet was forbidden them until the close of the seventeenth century, and they were confined to hoods and broad-brimmed protective hats, completely unadorned and severely practical.

Hat styles had proliferated since the late sixteenth century. Philip Stubbes, the Puritan pamphleteer, denounced in his *Anatomie of Abuses* (1583) the many varieties of hat that roused his disapproval, particularly when worn by the rowdy elements of his society. 'Sometimes', he claimed,

> they use them sharpe on the crowne, peaking up like the spire or shaft of a steeple, standing a quarter of a yard above the crowne of their heads; some lesse, as please the fantasies of their inconstant mindes. Othersome be flat and broade on the crowne, like the battlements of a house. Another sorte have rounde crownes, sometimes with one kind of bande, sometimes with another; now black, now white, now russed, now redde, now green, now yellow; never content with one colour or fashion two daies to an end. And as the fashions be rare and strange, so is the stuffe wherof their hattes be made divers also, silk, velvet, taffetie, sarsnet, woil, and what is more curious, some of a certaine kinde of fine haire, these they call bever hattes of X, XX, or XL shillings price, fetched from beyonde the seas, from whence a great sorte of other vanities doe come besides, and so common a thing it is that every serving man, counterman and other, even all indifferently, doe weare of these hattes, for he is of no account or estimation among men, if he have not a velvet or taffetie hat, and that must be pinched, and cunningly carved of the best fashion.

Charles I wore a plain hat with high sides and a slightly rounded crown, called, for obvious reasons, a chimneypot hat. It was made of the finest beaver hairs imported

from Canada and expensively treated to give the hat a rich but understated surface glow. He wore it when he was brought before the High Commission in Westminster Hall and refused to remove it in the presence of a self-constituted tribunal. He also wore it to the scaffold and thereby killed off the fashion for high-crowned hats for over a century – much as the high-brimmed hat of the Elizabethan noblewoman had been swept from the fashion stage when the Queen's laundress, Mrs Turner, wore one to her execution at Tyburn. Nevertheless, the status of the high hat had a universal appeal and it kept coming back. The high hat was even the choice of the Puritans (they called it the sugar-loaf), though it was by no means a practical form of headgear. In 1653 John Bulwer asked in *Anthropometamorphosis: Man Transformed*, 'What were our sugar-loofe hats, so mightily affected of late by men and women so incommodious for us that every puffe of wind deprived us of them, requiring the employment of one hand to keep them on?'

For once, it was women who abandoned the fashion first. Ned Ward, a fashionable satirist of the early eighteenth century, has a lady say to her husband:

> 'I verily believe you'd have me go
> In high-crowned hat and coif, like Gammer Crow'.

Scorn of this kind consigned the high hat to the rude and rustic world of the unfashionable country dweller. Similarly amused contempt surfaces in Dryden's comedy *The Wild Gallant*, when the heroine insults a sailor's wife by calling her 'steeplehat'. Nothing was more calculated to kill a fashion than an insult from the stage and, apart from nineteenth-century riding hats, women were never again to wear high crowns, so completely had the style become identified with old-fashioned, country plainness.

The broad-brimmed hats worn by the Cavaliers in England and the Musketeers in France in the seventeenth century were impressive but not particularly practical. Their large brims flopped down and were constantly in need of 'cocking' in order not to obscure the wearer's vision. The hats of the courts of Louis XIV and Charles II were magnificent; deep gold lace edged their brims and their crowns were buried in feathers. But their days were numbered. The advance of the periwig soon made

The cocked hat, or tricorne, the most popular hat of the 18th century, worn here by General Kléber, one of Napoleon's generals.

such hats impossible to wear. Their place was taken by the characteristic hat of the eighteenth century – the cocked hat, or tricorne. This was worn by gentlemen and courtiers across Europe and copied by the lower-middle classes, clerks and artisans.

The tricorne was essentially a fashionable town hat worn for show. In fact, the ultra-smart, who could not bear to risk dislodging their wigs or showering their shoulders with powder, carried the hat, rather than wearing it. But, on the head or in the hand, the cut, depth and type of cock was crucial. Sharp-eyed and giving no quarter, the fashionable young men who lounged in the arcades of the Palais Royale and paraded in St James's mercilessly mocked any would-be man of fashion who got the minutest detail wrong. Even before Exquisites, Macaronis and Incroyables – who brought fashionable dress to a fever-pitch of fetishism – gentlemen lavished more care on their hats and wigs than on any other item of clothing, knowing that these accessories, above all, reflected how up-to-date they were.

John Sly, 'Haberdasher of Hats and Tobacconist', placed an advertisement in the *Spectator* pointing out that he was

> preparing hats for the several kinds of heads that make figures in the realm of Great Britain, with cocks significant of their powers and faculties. His hats for men of the faculties of law and physic do but just turn up to give a little life to their sagacity; his military hats glare full in the face; and he has prepared a familiar easy cock for all good companions between the above-mentioned extremes.

Of the necessity for 'cocking' the wide brims of the seventeenth-century hat there can be no doubt. Quite apart from the dramatic effect on hats of the burgeoning craze for wigs, brims were too large for practicality or safety. The first step had been to pin them on the right side so that a man could, at least, swing his sword arm properly. The next stage had been to pin up all three sides so that a man galloping hard would not lose his hat or risk losing his seat while trying to hold his hat on.

Like any other fashionable item of dress, the tricorne, once established, subdivided itself into different styles, each of which was fiercely defended by the fashionable young men of the time, until the next style came along and made it hopelessly *déclassé*. The earliest 'cock', the Monmouth Cock, which turned up at the back brim, was superseded by the Ramillies cock, commemorating the Battle of Ramillies. This was succeeded by a larger German 'cock' called the Kevenhüller, after Field Marshal Ludwig Andreas Khevenhüller, commander of Prince Eugene of Austria's dragoons. The Kevenhüller was the most popular and enduring cock of all. By 1760, as a newspaper article of the time explains, hats were worn by the fashionable

> upon an average six inches and three fifths broad in the brim, and cocked between Quaker and Kevenhüller. Some have their hats open before them like a church spout, or the scales they weigh flour in, some wear them rather sharper like the nose of a greyhound, and we can distinguish, by the cock of the hat, the mode of the wearer's mind. There is the military cock and the mercantile cock; and while the beaux of St James's wear their hats under their arms, the beaux of Moorfields Mall wear them diagonally over the left or right eye. Some wear their hats with the corners, which should come over their forehead, in a direct line pointing into the air. . . . Others do not but half cover their heads, which is indeed owing to the shallowness of their crowns.

Clearly, such a universally followed fashion had to fall from grace and, indeed, the cocked hat was pulled down by the Nivernois which was all the rage by 1770. Named after Louis-Jules Mancini Mazarin, Duke of Nivernois, it was extremely small and its flaps fastened by hooks and eyes up to a shallow crown that was seen above them. It was a case of *reductio ad absurdum* and the style was doomed. Round hats were reinstated as smart morning wear and the French Revolution completed the downfall of the three-cornered hat on both sides of the Channel and across the Atlantic. For formal occasions and uniform wear, it was succeeded by the ponderous bicorne which laid few claims to stylishness and had a pomposity entirely fitting the attitudes of the newly emerging man who preferred power to prettiness, sobriety to sensationalism and law-making to licentiousness. It was almost inevitable that it would become Napoleon's signature hat.

It was in the late seventeenth century that women's headwear began to create its own fashion without shadowing or echoing the developments in men's hats. Millinery was now an independent art form, confined solely to the making of women's hats. First recorded in 1529, the term referred to artefacts for which Milan and the regions of northern Italy had become famous, including ribbons, gloves and cutlery. But the product most sought after was the fine straw hat, and the haberdashers who imported them were known as Millaners, a word which gradually became corrupted to the modern form. By 1679 millinery was the accepted word for all female headwear, although, for the next century and more, a milliner was as much a dressmaker as a maker of hats.

For the larger part of the eighteenth century women's hats joined men's in the battle with the wig. But it was an uneven contest. So completely had the wig taken over the fashionable mind that hats, when worn at all, were seen only as very secondary fashion statements. The most popular style was flat, usually in straw, and either small with a slight brim or more substantial with a wider brim. It sat uncomfortably atop the powdered wig rather like a dinner plate, worn either completely flat or angled to dip towards the brow.

For ordinary women the mob cap was the most attractive form of headdress, made possible by the invention of tulle in 1768. Essentially an inexpensive, modest

Below left The flat straw hat of the late 18th century, illustration from *La Parure des Dames*; *below* Mob cap, 1780.

Two of the many millinery styles of the late 18th century: *Top* Chapeau à l'indienne; *above* Chapeau cloche; 1798.

Alfred, Count D'Orsay, the Parisian dandy, wearing the fashionable top hat of the early 19th century, 1834.

covering that almost totally eclipsed the hair, it remained until well into the nineteenth century and can, in its all-enveloping qualities, be seen as the precursor of the poke bonnet. Caps of all sizes and volume were still popular in the second half of the nineteenth century, from the demure cap of lace wired into the shape of a butterfly and worn perched above the forehead, to the Ranelagh mob, which, despite being described in the *London Chronicle* of 1762 as consisting of 'a piece of gauze . . . clouted above the head, then crossed under the chin, and brought back to fasten behind, the two ends hanging down like a pair of pigeons' tails', remained popular for over a hundred years.

As the wig gradually disappeared, so the variety of millinery styles increased: large, small; tilted forward, pushed to the sides or worn on the back of the head; deep-crowned, wide-brimmed; hats with large wide crowns pleated into a waist, hats with tall narrow crowns pulled up vertically; soft crowns, flower-pot crowns; the list is almost endless. They came in silk, beaver, straw, gauze and chip. They were adorned with bows, ostrich feathers, ribbon hatbands and lace. But perhaps the most extraordinary style of all (which also pointed towards the poke bonnet) was the calash, a large folding hood, made of silk and built upon arches of cane tall enough to clear the height of the coiffure. Usually of green cambric, it became a fashion in the United States as well as in Europe, and a writer from Philadelphia hit upon the allure of a contraption which to modern eyes seems graceless and cumbersome when he described it as 'looking down a green lane to see a rose blooming at the end'. John Watson, in his *Annals of Philadelphia*, published in 1829, when hat extravagance had quietened down, also pointed out that all women in the city wore caps; a bare head, he averred, was never seen. It was equally true of Europe. The hegemony of the hair had been challenged. For the next 125 years no woman who had any pretensions to decency, quite apart from fashion-consciousness, would be seen in public without a complete and proper headcovering.

In the nineteenth century the world of fashion was, for the first time, arbitrated by the middle classes. Middle-class man saw himself as the cynosure of seriousness, a role that required a hat with presence and stature. So the high-crowned hat returned, soon to dominate the century as the top hat, but at this stage a felt hat with tall sides and a rounded crown. As with all male dress in the early nineteenth century, it came from the country gentleman. In this instance he had narrowed the brim of his hat for riding and, to minimize the risk of injury if thrown, had raised the crown so that it would act as a rudimentary crash helmet. As a hunting hat it was a triumph of practicality. To keep it on the head even when taking fences, an inner band contained a drawstring that could be pulled tight. It became the general all-purpose male hat and would no doubt have remained so if a new invention and a boldly original approach to scale had not toppled it from its fashion pinnacle.

The first tall 'silk' hat was made in Paris. A highly polished beaver, it looked so much like satin that it was called silk beaver. The hat was introduced to London in the 1790s by John Hetherington, a hatter in Charing Cross, who created 'hatter's plush', a very fine silk shag applied to a felt base to give the hat the appearance of being made of silk. It is said that when Hetherington first appeared in Whitehall wearing his tall shiny black hat he caused a riot. Laughter turned to anger and he was pelted with whatever the crowd could lay its hands on. He survived and so did his plush hat – which became *the* headwear of authority for the next century.

Yet it was a fashion that always had its detractors. The 'top hat' question was a perennial favourite in the letter columns of periodicals and magazines. A letter to the *Hatters' Gazette* asking, 'Can any single plea be urged for retaining so absurd a hat? Is it comfortable? Surely not, for every man discards it as soon as he is out of London. Is it convenient? Neither on the head or off,' is typical of many. But it took more than letters to shake nineteenth-century ideas of propriety and the top hat was too firmly entrenched as a hat of power to be easily superseded.

Lock's of St James's named their hat styles after the customers for whom they were created. The bowler which they designed and sold in 1850, at a cost of twelve shillings, to William Coke of Norfolk, they called a Coke hat. It was actually made, however, by the Bowler family of Southwark and gradually took their name as its popularity grew. The bowler was the first hard, round-crowned hat. William Coke had ordered it to overcome the problem of having constantly to replace his gamekeeper's soft hats before they were worn out because they were so easily damaged. He wanted a hat as rigid as a top hat but not so tall. Coke tested Lock's solution by standing on its crown. It bore his weight; he bought; and a style that has lasted until today was born. Frequently misnamed, the Coke, or bowler, is not a billy- or bully-cock hat, though it has often been assumed to be so. A billycock was originally an eighteenth-century cocked hat beloved of urban 'bullies' whose great joy was disturbing the peace. It was also the name of a hard-crowned Cornish miner's hat created by a local hatmaker, William Cock. It was merely the similarity of the names Cock and Coke that caused confusion over the naming of this quintessentially English hat style – a style that was associated with the city gent, who wore it in black; the racecourse 'bookie', who favoured brown; and, in the United States, where it was known as the 'derby', was popular with all classes of tradesmen and artisans. It has proved to be one of the most enduring and successful hats ever designed.

If the nineteenth century saw men go hard-hatted both literally and metaphorically, it witnessed a helterskelter of constantly changing styles for women. Firmly entrenched as the decorative sex, they made fashion a central part of their existence. Having done so, they created a hydra-headed monster that needed constantly to

Early 20th-century caricature, 'La Mode *c.* 1910'.

renew itself. The rate of fashion change speeded up as the century progressed so that, by the late 1880s, styles appeared and disappeared with such bewildering speed that only the most dedicated of fashion followers could keep up. Supply created demand and, in order to satisfy the need for the new, milliners forced their imaginations to range back and forth across the centuries, pillaging past eras for fresh ideas. It was not the way to create good – or even memorable – fashion and despite the plethora of variations played on the theme of nineteenth-century women's headwear, it is extremely difficult to discern any true stylistic differences.

The poke bonnet appeared in such a wide variety of shapes, sizes, fabrics and colours, under so many different names, that to pinpoint a particular style is virtually impossible. One year the brim would be small, the next large and the following enormous. It would closely hug the cheeks one season and flare away from them the next. The crown would be high in some years and low in others. By 1826 the bonnet had become huge, its size exaggerated by the flowers, ribbons and plumes that almost submerged it. Five years later, everything had slid towards the back of the head, only to spend the following five in coming forward again.

Although well-off women wore bonnets in the finest Swiss or Italian straw, most were made of plaited straw. This was a cheap material, well suited to those with more fashion sense than money. Imitation straw was also used, made from paper, cardboard, grass and horsehair. The second half of the nineteenth century saw the introduction of felt for women's hats, along with velvet and tulle. The 'drawn silk' bonnet was an especial favourite, ruched and gathered in flattering folds. Throughout the whole century, however, the success of a bonnet depended on its trim. Rather than throw away a hat with plenty of life left in it simply because the colour of ribbons or flowers had become *passé*, women retrimmed their bonnets to fit the new season's fashions. Most trims were placed inside the brim, their colours chosen to match the lining and, like it, to create a frame for the face.

The bonnet's shape and size were also affected by changes in hairstyles. When the hair was high and dressed in complicated ringlets, the bonnet dwindled to a tiny cap-like device perched high on the back or hanging over the forehead. When hair became smoother and less voluminous, the bonnet expanded to fill the vacuum.

The flat hat, the early form of the Edwardian platter, on which ravishing mounds of flowers, leaves, butterflies and birds could be displayed, developed with the same jerky inconsistency as the bonnet. Again, desperately searching for novelty, milliners looked back and took devices and details from all periods of history, especially the Middle Ages. The results were a confused mish-mash of decorative styles that, in their fussiness and inconsequentiality, showed how thoroughly women's fashion had lost its way. It was only as the new century dawned that the confusion began to clear, ready for the Great War, which was to change fashion radically and permanently and pave the way for the modern, twentieth-century hat.

Thomas Gainsborough, *The Morning Walk*, 1785.

HEADS
IN FLOWER

No designer's élan can outclass the natural
style of hats created by individuals either as a
special expression of their personality or in
response to ceremonial needs. Such hats are
nearly always made with flowers — often
freshly picked and arranged artlessly on the
head like a bouquet. These beautiful examples
from Senegal and New Zealand could grace
the smartest wedding or garden party and
would probably outshine any examples of the
milliner's art that might also be on show.
That being said, it must be admitted that
Christian Lacroix's superb creation is their
equal.

Above Hat by Christian Lacroix, 1980s

Opposite Senegal, 1980

18   *Right* New Zealand Maori

PHILIP TREACY

*Only occasionally does a fashion talent
emerge that is so in tune with the spirit of
the time that it is instantly and universally
hailed. Such a talent belongs to Philip
Treacy, the young Irishman who has
become a world famous milliner with
dizzying speed since graduating from
London's Royal College of Art in 1990.
His hats have been described as dauntingly
original and they are certainly not for the
woman who is in any sense unsure of
herself. It is indicative of their
uncompromising design statement that they
invariably look at their most stunning
when worn by one of the world's top
models, such as Linda Evangelista, shown
here wearing a feathered creation from
Treacy's Spring/Summer 1992 collection.*

*Treacy's hats make a statement about
modern fashion and contemporary ideas of
elegance that will be of great interest to
future fashion historians. Their
exaggerated scale and outlandish shapes
echo the theatricality of current fashion
and convey to perfection the* fin-de-siècle
mood of the 1990s.

Philip Treacy, Spring/Summer 1992 collection,
photo by Irving Penn

YVES SAINT LAURENT

Overleaf
*Beautiful millinery deserves beautiful
photography. These 1985 hats by Yves
Saint Laurent have been photographed by
David Seidner with the sensitivity and
understanding that is the greatest homage
one artist can pay to another. The result is
a diptych of true grace.*

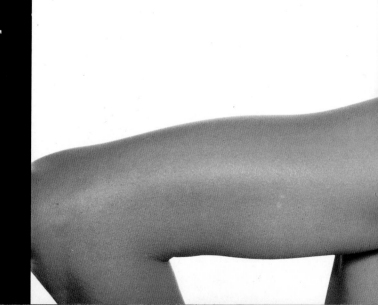

*H*ats are the most unnatural of all items of clothing; they are the least necessary but the most powerful. Their semiotics are frequently complex but always clear. They are the tools of transformation and authority. This is why power and ceremony are normally hatted.

Royalty has always needed imposing trappings in order to hide as effectively as possible the fact that kings are only men. When William Makepeace Thackeray said of George IV that he was 'but a bow and a grin; take him to pieces and find – some clothes and then nothing,' he could have been describing most hereditary monarchs for the last five hundred years. Kings have always relied heavily on the ornamental accessories of their role to induce in their subjects the 'willing suspension of disbelief' that is the basis of their hold on power. And of course the most potent symbol of that power is the crown.

But even in the most totalitarian of courts, such as those of Charlemagne, Henry VIII and Louis XIV, not all power can reside in the king or emperor. It must be shared – and so must its symbol. The crown, too valuable and inconvenient for any but the most rigidly formal occasions, must find an everyday substitute which can assume equal importance. The hat serves this function. Power fears informality, but a hat imparts decorum and seriousness to the most run-of-the-mill face, as Holbein's drawings of Tudor courtiers make clear. Even when they were merely being sketched, courtiers wore formal headwear to indicate that they held a position of privilege and authority. The flat velvet caps of the men and the stiffly formal coifs of the women were deeply symbolic of their class, and were worn as proof of their wearers' eminence.

Covering the head for protection was a consideration for only the lowest labourers. For everyone else, the hat was a mark of status. That was the true reason why men and women of all classes covered their heads. It showed their estate and allowed them to give and receive what was known as hat honour.

Hat honour was a vital prop to the status quo. It spread outwards and downwards from the court. Kings expected those surrounding them to show respect for the throne by uncovering their heads when the monarch arrived in their midst. Courtiers demanded the same recognition from their immediate inferiors, such as the gentlemen pages and the sons of minor aristocrats who served them. These in turn expected hat honour from their inferiors. Everybody but the king had someone to doff to and – apart from the very lowest classes of society – someone who must doff to them. Each doffing was an acknowledgment of the chain of power that held society together – a chain that began with the crown.

Helmet of the Household Cavalry, a piece of military headgear whose use is now purely ceremonial.

It was, of course, a serious breach of etiquette for a subject to wear a hat in the presence of a king. The corollary to this was that for a man to be granted the privilege to do this was a rare and much-prized honour. Henry VIII was not only a fashion leader, he was also a stickler for the protocol of dress. So it was a notable concession when he decreed that 'our trusty and well-beloved subject Walter Copinger is so dis-eased in his head that . . . we have by these presents licens'd him to use and wear his bonnet upon his solid head . . . as well in our presence as elsewhere, at his liberty.'

A precedent for such royal magnanimity had already been set by King John who, more than a century earlier, rewarded John de Courcy, Earl of Ulster, for gallantry. When King John was summoned by Philip II of France either to trial or to combat for the murder of Prince Arthur, he appointed de Courcy to undertake the combat for his country's honour. Philip's champion was so terrified of de Courcy that he ran away. The two kings, robbed of their spectacle, urged de Courcy to give them a display of his strength. Placing his helmet on a tree stump, the champion cleaved it with a terrific blow that so impressed John that he declared, 'Never unvail thy bonnet again, before king or subject.' The privilege was passed down through each generation of de Courcys. The etiquette they established was to remain hatted while others uncovered and then to remove their hats separately in order to keep alive their unique privilege without being guilty of lèse-majesté. The privilege was abused only once, in the reign of George III, when the de Courcy of the time remained hatted throughout an audience with the king. The rebuke was tart, hitting at de Courcy's right to be considered a true gentleman: 'The gentleman', the king said loudly, 'has a right to be covered before me; but even King John could give him no right to be covered before ladies.'

There were, of course, many commoners who found it demeaning to be expected to uncover before royalty and none reacted more strongly against the custom than those for whom loyalty to king was as nothing compared with respect for God. The question as to whether or not the head should be covered in church was a problem for men in many religions and in most Western countries. Even the clergy seemed uncertain as to how to treat headwear in or out of church.

Covered and uncovered heads in church. William Hogarth, plate 2 of 'The Industrious 'Prentice', 1747.

It was straightforward vanity and temporal pride, however, that motivated Thomas Wolsey's actions in the reign of Henry VIII, when he was made a cardinal by the pope. The Thirteenth General Council, held in Lyons in 1245 by Innocent IV, decreed that, as a special distinction, cardinals should wear a red hat. The colour was to be a reminder that they must be prepared to shed their blood, as Christ had shed his, for the liberty of Christian peoples. Up to this time only pontiffs had worn red so the Council of Lyons enhanced the status of cardinals within the Church. It was an honour of which they were very conscious – none of them more so than Wolsey. As Leigh Hunt records, the pope sent the hat 'without any state or show, through the hands of an ordinary messenger' but Wolsey had the messenger 'stayed by the way', dressed in rich apparel, sent back to Dover and met there by a 'grand and gorgeous cavalcade of prelates and gentry' who accompanied him and the hat in triumph to London. There it was 'placed on a sideboard full of plate, with lighted tapers round about it and the greatest dukes in the lande must make courtesie thereto'.

The cardinal's hat, with its pendant tassels said to be copied from the headgear of the priests in the Temple of Juno, was the most overtly 'showy' hat in the Catholic

Church, apart from the pontiff's mitre. Such showiness was not found in other religions. In fact many religions, especially nonconformist sects, did not set aside any garment for specific use by their clergy.

Quaker dress, for example, is largely a survival of clothing common in the time of Charles II from which all decoration has been removed. William Penn, asked by Charles II for a symbolic difference between his hat and that of the Quakers replied, 'My hat is plain, thine is adorned with ribbons and feathers. The only difference in our religions lies in the ornaments that have been added to thine.'

In 1669 Penn wrote a treatise against raising the hat to any but the Lord ('No Cross, No Crown; or Several Solid Reasons Against Hat Honour . . .). One 'solid reason' ran as follows: 'The hat choketh because it telleth tales; it telleth what men are . . . it is blowing of a trumpet.' A story is told that when Penn kept his hat on in the presence of Charles II, the king removed his own. When he was asked why, the king reminded Penn that only one person might keep his hat on in the royal presence.

George Fox, the founder of the Quaker Movement, wore a hat identical to that of his monarch, except that it had no feather. In 1656 he had refused to take it off in the presence of magistrates at Launceston Assizes, with the stirring words, 'Proud flesh looks for hat honour. When the Lord sent me forth into the world he forbad me to put off my hat to any, high or low.'

Hats were important to Quakers of both sexes and often caused contention. George Fox disapproved of all hats for women, especially what he called the 'skimming dish hat', by which he meant any hat with an immodestly wide brim. He preferred Quaker women to wear hoods – known variously as cardinals, capuchins or riding hoods – as being best able to preserve their piety and modesty by totally covering the hair. Hoods had in fact been a common Quaker headcovering: a meeting held in Southwark, London, in 1707, entered into the records the complaint that 'several women Friends do usually hang their riding-hoods on the rail of the gallery so low that Friends that sit under the gallery are incommoded'.

After Fox's outburst, Quaker women first compromised by wearing the skimming-dish hat on top of their hoods. But eventually, despite male disapproval, they left the hoods off altogether. By the first years of the Revolution, John Watson in his *Annals of Philadelphia* could claim that all the women of that Quaker city wore large white beaver hats with very shallow crowns, secured to the head by silk cords tied under the chin.

It is, however, the bonnet that is the most characteristic item of female Quaker dress. Made of drab – a coarse linen or woollen cloth in beige or grey – it was known variously as the stiff-brim, the coal scuttle, the sugar-scoop and the poke bonnet. The 1820 memorandum book of Ennion Cook of Chester County, Pennsylvania, states that it was 'Martha Routh, a Minister of the Gospel from Old England', who introduced the bonnet to American Friends at a meeting at Goshen, Pennsylvania, in 1798. It was a standard shape on which many variations were played. According to the way in which it was folded and plaited, it reflected the attitudes of the various meeting houses after which it was named. The English Quaker bonnet was not plaited but gathered; it had a cape at the back and flared out at the front.

The beliefs of the socio-religious group the Shakers, founded in the eighteenth century, were based on the fundamental doctrines of purity, community and separation of the sexes. For Shakers, work was worship. Shaker men originally wore broad-brimmed, low-crowned hats of fur and wool but after the American Civil War they adopted straw hats for the summer, keeping their fur hats for Sabbath wear and their wool hats for everyday winter dress. Shaker women started out with a close-fitting cap of linen or wool, or, in rural areas, a small flat hat of chip (a straw substitute, made of shaved wood), covered in black silk, with a brim six inches wide. But by 1805 they had adopted Quaker bonnets as a more practical style. These were made of pasteboard covered with silk until around 1830, when they began to be made from palm leaves imported from Cuba. The Civil War disrupted those supplies and straw became the universal material of the Shaker bonnet for the rest of the nineteenth century. Straw bonnets were still being worn as late as the 1920s.

Religious sects are reluctant to allow variations in their members' dress because the strength of the movement frequently rests on the denial of individuality and the subjugation of personal choice. Fashion frightens them because it is synonymous with change and individual responses to such change, both of which they frequently see as a threat. The same is true in many areas of public life where traditions are used to bolster positions that, if questioned, might seem untenable. Hats have frequently been the cause of – or at least the excuse for – political disagreement, especially as to when and how they might be worn. The 'hats-on or hats-off' controversy has not only preoccupied religious observance, it has also rumbled at various levels across political history. When Peter Stuyvesant in his capacity as governor of New Amsterdam made his inaugural speech, he did so with his head uncovered while his audience stood for the hour-long oration with their hats on. Their covered heads, unlike the conventions in Europe, were a mark of respect to him and his position, just as his bare head was a sign of his superiority and importance. American egalitarianism came to the fore a little later at the Continental Congress of 23 December 1789, at Annapolis, Maryland. The Congress was held at a crucial juncture in American history. Many of the states were so exhausted after the War of Independence and so disillusioned with the idea of central government after their experiences with Britain that they did not even bother to send representatives. It was, therefore, vitally important that the central political role of Congress should be acknowledged. A ceremony was arranged to mark George Washington's resignation as commander-in-chief of the army. Returning to the earlier convention, a committee, including Thomas Jefferson, agreed that during Washington's address members of Congress would remain seated and keep their hats on. They would refuse him the honour of rising and the courtesy of baring their heads so that when he had finished his address and acknowledged the authority of Congress, they could

Shakers near Lebanon. Note the bonnet of women members and the broadbrimmed hats of Shaker men.

reinforce the power of the assembly over that of the individual by only then briefly raising their hats to him while remaining seated. The decision marked an important watershed in American politics.

In his *Hats of Humanity*, George Augustus Sala describes a visit by the Whig politician Charles James Fox to Napoleon in Paris after the Peace of Amiens. The Emperor, 'wishing to show marked courtesy to his distinguished visitor, would not suffer him to retain his hat, as was then the courtly custom, in his hand but took it himself and placed it on a side table.' Napoleon, though originally a revolutionary, soon adopted a form of hat that became a clear symbol of his power. Like the rest of his carefully contrived dress, it had been chosen to help give him legitimacy within the courts of hereditary kings and authority over citizens and generals alike. In fact, even before Napoleon emerged, the leaders within revolutionary France had distanced themselves from the mobs who had brought them to power and had adopted the headgear of the gentleman. Robespierre favoured a tall 'sugar loaf' turned up with dark blue silk; the characteristic hat of Danton, Callot d'Herbois and Herbert and Camille Desmoulins was the steeple crown, and the Republican generals were distinguished by their 'monstrous flapped hats, surmounted by tufts of tri-coloured feathers'. The old adage that 'You cannot lead a revolution in a top hat' is undoubtedly true, but equally so is the fact that once the revolution is over, you cannot lead a government in a Phrygian cap.

The Phrygian cap, the soft, conical hat given to Greeks and Roman slaves when they became freemen, is traditionally considered to be the 'cap of liberty'. It and the top hat typify the two groups into which political hats have fallen in the past. The high, hard hat represented the power of political conservatism and the rule of the status quo; the soft hat was the symbol of the outsider who, at worst, wished to destroy society or, at best, refused to abide by its rules. In the nineteenth century, when hard hats were the headwear of power, soft hats alarmed the authorities but often gained approval from the masses. When Lajos Kossuth, the Hungarian patriot, toured England and the United States in 1851 he caused a sensation – not so much by his words and actions as by his hats. Here was an authoritative national figure who eschewed the top hat and wore instead a dashing soft hat of great Romantic appeal. The Kossuth hat – later adopted by the Irish nationalists, the Fenians – became a runaway fashion in America. In fact, in 1852 it was being suggested in the trade that the soft felt hat had entirely extinguished high crowns in the United States. Although this was an exaggeration, it was nonetheless true that soft felts were more popular in America than anywhere in Europe.

A few years later, Garibaldi, the father of Italian unity, also captured the imagination of United States citizens with his broad-brimmed, soft-crowned hat that he was believed to have copied, as a conscious political gesture, from the field hat of the Italian peasant. However, a contemporary American writer claimed that Garibaldi had 'picked up his "pork pie" hat during his campaigns in South America, precisely as his red flannel shirt was borrowed from the ordinary attire of the American merchant seaman.' Regardless of its origins, the hat was used by Garibaldi as a symbol of radical, independent thought, and the slouch hat became the badge of the idealist. It also became the favourite hat of painters and poets who knew that to have any credibility at all creativity must strike at the status quo, startle the bourgeoisie and force radical reappraisal of artistic beliefs.

Nineteenth-century North American attitudes to dress were more liberal and

Detail from 19th-century cartoon showing Garibaldi recommending to the Pope the Phrygian cap, symbol of liberty and democracy.

The Autograph Collector (1933), cartoon by David Low depicting Anthony Eden as an ineffectual appeaser of Hitler and Mussolini.

pragmatic than those current in Britain and Europe. Even after 1848, the year of revolutions, American politicians were less hidebound in their choice of hats than were their counterparts across the Atlantic. Individuality in hat styles was permitted to presidential candidates with a freedom not accorded to would-be prime ministers. From Washington's cocked hat to Lincoln's old silk stovepipe – made for him by George Hall of Springfield, Illinois, and worn, as a result of the President's notorious lack of interest in his appearance, until its shabbiness embarrassed his supporters – individuality in hats was part of any presidential campaign.

In modern times, Franklin D. Roosevelt's fedora became in his campaigning years as famous as the man himself. Dwight D. Eisenhower made history when he appeared at his inauguration wearing not the traditional top hat but a homburg. However, John F. Kennedy, who had campaigned hatless during his presidential year, gave in to tradition and attended his inauguration in a black silk top hat.

The dullness and predictability of politicians' hats on the other side of the Atlantic may be judged by the fact that Prime Minister Anthony Eden's essentially boring black homburg became fashion news in the 1930s. Its colour caused as much comment as its untraditional shape and cost, which at two guineas was considerable. However, it would be a mistake to assume that hats were of no political significance in Europe. As long ago as the eighteenth century, Sweden's political parties had been given popular names by their followers according to their foreign policies. The Hats or Hattar – so called because they wore three-cornered officer's hats – wished to go to war against Russia to regain territory lost at the Peace of Nystad in 1721; the opposition party, nicknamed the Caps or Mussorna, preferred to preserve peace. In 1932, as part of his attempt to create unity in the Fascist Party of Italy, Mussolini decreed that all party members must wear an Alpine fur hat.

But, predictably, it was in the formal and rule-conscious world of British politics that hats were of utmost importance. The satirical cry, 'Oh! What a shocking bad hat!', which became a catchphrase in the nineteenth century, reputedly originated with a parliamentary candidate who, instead of directly bribing voters, buttonholed them and said, 'What a shocking bad hat you are wearing, my man. Call at my warehouse and you shall have a new one, free.' On election day, to expose the corruption, the opposition chanted, 'Oh! What a shocking bad hat!' The cry spread like wildfire.

Throughout the nineteenth century, the hat of power was the topper, worn by politicians, professional men, anyone who considered himself a gentleman and those, such as undertakers, who required a hat that would give them the solemn and important *appearance* of being a gentleman. Such an obviously 'boss-class' item of clothing could not help but arouse controversy and, almost from its invention, the top hat had its vociferous detractors as well as its staunch supporters. A poem published in the London magazine *Truth* in 1886 began 'I hate it!' The rival publication, the *Globe*, immediately published an answering piece of doggerel beginning 'I love it!' As with most 'posh' fashion, the attitudes expressed told more about society – its divisions and class attitudes – than about the hat itself. The top hat was certainly imposing. Equally certainly, it was uncomfortable to wear – like much status clothing. Those privileged to use it felt that the glory outweighed the discomfort; those debarred did all in their power to denigrate it. The popular press took up the cause, each publication following the line it felt would be most likely to appeal to the prejudices of its readers. An editorial in the *Daily News* pointed out that, if the top hat was no longer appropriate to daily life, then it was merely part of a capitalist dress that was becoming increasingly unjustifiable. 'Given the frock coat and trousers', it claimed, 'the tall hat follows. Reform must begin with the dress in general and level up to the hats.' The editorial elicited a letter addressed from the Oxford and Cambridge Club which suggested that ' "Chimney pots" make people look like gentlemen' – which was, of course, why socialists disliked them. It continued, 'Some of us object to look like brigands, plough boys, Cavaliers and Roundheads, Turks, planters of South Carolina or High Church curates, not to mention Quakers, coal heavers and policemen.... Imagine such men as the Duke of Wellington, Sir Robert Peel, Lord Eversley and many more of the same stamp in pot hats and ulsters.' An American correspondent joined the debate, calling the gentleman's tall stiff hat 'his little black household and society God. He cannot travel, cannot go anywhere where he is to be on parade without it.'

If political hats are about power and allegiance, this is even more true of military headwear. The wearing of military uniform is intended to foster the group loyalty that is an important part of a disciplined fighting force. Pride in the regiment produces pride in the individual, and pride – so runs the theory – overcomes fear. If a soldier can also share in the pride and power of his leader, so much the better. That is why Mussolini, who habitually wore the fez, imposed it on the officers of the Italian army in the 1920s.

Modern warfare demands an efficient working uniform but, even so, the importance of ceremonial is not forgotten. For this reason, all regiments in the world make a distinction between working and dress uniforms. The former are essentially practical, the latter are for show. For battle, total efficiency is vital. The head must be protected in the most effective way possible. The design of helmets is therefore universally similar. For everyday wear, most armies favour the beret or a soft, informal fatigue hat. It is ceremonial wear that allows scope for regimental differences, largely based on their individual histories. Here practicality gives way to theatricality, and modernity to atavism. Considerable flamboyance is permitted. Nothing could be more inappropriate to modern military life than the British guardsman's bearskin (it was not especially practical even when first introduced in 1815) or the Italian Bersaglieri's wide-brimmed hat extravagantly trimmed with gleaming cockerel feathers. Yet both are worn with pride. Romanticism is what ceremonial uniform is all about, and most regimental dress uniform, including hats,

Member of the Imperial Guard of Napoleon I, 1809–1815. From an engraving by F. Bastin.

harks back to the past, with soldiers wearing items of clothing (such as swords) that have absolutely no meaning in modern military life.

In all armies, modern ceremonial dress harks back to the military dress of the eighteenth century because it was at that time that most countries initiated their permanent, centrally controlled standing armies of volunteer recruits. Most European and American regiments were influenced by the Prussian army of Frederick the Great – the first army to have a totally standardized uniform even down to the shoe buckles – although initially, in the United States, uniforms were an ad-hoc measure until the Continental Congress of 1775 laid down permanent dress codes. It was George Washington who decided that U.S. army officers must wear coloured cockades in their hats in order to show their rank clearly: red or pink for field officers, yellow or buff for captains and green for subalterns.

The cocked hat was the standard masculine headwear in the eighteenth century and it was worn by officers in most countries as part of their uniform. The tricorne – the French called it the Androsmane, the English and Americans knew it as the Kevenhüller – was *the* masculine style until the bicorne began to supplant it in the 1790s. The bicorne had the advantage that it could be folded flat and carried under the arm; hence its popular name of *chapeau bras*. It remained an item of ceremonial dress for high-ranking officers in the U.S., French and English navies until well into the twentieth century and is still a part of court and diplomatic dress.

The cocked hat died out as military headdress because, for all its style, it was not practical in battle. It was replaced by the Hungarian shako which was first adopted by the Prussian army in the early eighteenth century and then copied by most European armies and some American regiments. A truncated cone, the shako was peaked and usually had a plume or pom-pom. It was frequently covered in bearskin and offered a fair degree of protection, if not much comfort. It was in turn supplanted by the kepi, which was introduced by the French army in 1861. In effect a cut-down shako, its distinctive flat top sometimes sloped towards the front. Taken up in Europe and the United States, it made little impact on British military headwear. In America it vied for military popularity for many years with the broad-brimmed felt Kossuth, known variously as the 'Hardee', 'Jeff Davis' or 'M'Clellan' and described by a contemporary writer as 'a brigand-looking affair, decidedly conical, and with a slightly slouched brim'. It was a style very similar to those worn by cowboys and imparted a certain louche masculinity to the wearer.

The kepi was more decorous, but even this simple hat could be customized. In 1864, James Landregan, of the 42nd Pennsylvanian Volunteers, finding his cap rather dull, added a white 'bucktail' to copy the tail on the frontiersman's coonskin cap. His approving colonel, Thomas Kane, ordered all his men to do the same and announced that the regiment would in future be known as the Bucktails. It was one of the last examples of the military system allowing individual taste to manifest itself. Standardization of male dress, in civilian as well as military life, was making originality and eccentricity the sole province of women. As the nineteenth century progressed, men's hats dwindled to a handful of styles, while women's blossomed into a bewildering variety.

Tibetan monk in ceremonial headdress.

RELIGIOUS HATS

What distinguishes religious hats from headgear designed merely for protection or in response to fashion? They are sober, largely unornamented, and often have an upward emphasis that can be seen as symbolizing the soaring of the soul towards heaven. There is a serenity about them that marks them out from the hats worn every day. What could be purer than the fez (opposite below) worn by the Dervish dancer in Konya, Turkey? In its total lack of decoration it symbolizes the purity of the religious experience denoted by the man's expression. The calmness and gravity of the fez are reflected in the strength of the Pope's mitre (above left) and the elegant simplicity of the hat of the Tibetan priest (left).

Closer to the ordinary, but no less strong, is the Rastafarian's 'crown'. Like the Jewish skullcap, worn here by a worker in New York's garment district, it is serious but relaxed. Such hats suggest immediately that they belong to religious conviction rather than to the world of everyday.

Above left Pope Paul VI addressing the Synod, October 1969

Left Tibetan priest, Katmandu

Opposite top Jewish garment worker, New York

Opposite centre Rastafarian, London, 1991

Opposite bottom The Order of the Mevlevi, the Dervish dancers, Konya, Turkey

THE CROWN

Most enduring of all royal symbols, the crown has always stood apart from the vagaries of fashion. Its connotations are so powerful that it has never been able to make the leap from regalia to style. Attempts to make the crown into a hat shape always end up as nothing more than fancy dress, as this example from Vivienne Westwood's 1986/87 Queen Elizabeth II-inspired collection shows (opposite below). What Westwood's amusing version lacks is the dignity that the real thing automatically has when worn on a royal head. The crown of Upper and Lower Egypt (left) is impressive and even intimidating as a symbol of royal power but any attempt to translate it into modern fashion would render it merely ridiculous. The same is true of the magnificent crown on the head of J. L. Saler's Gilded Virgin *of 1750 (below left).*

But crowns do not have to rely on extravagance in order to have their effect. Napoleon chose to be crowned with an elegantly understated example, as did Frederick IV of Germany when he became Holy Roman Emperor in 1452. Precious stones, jewels, silver and gold make the point of kingship perfectly apparent without need for elaborate and superfluous additions.

Above left Crown of Upper and Lower Egypt, *c.* 1180 BC, from a wallpainting showing Ramesses III

Left J. L. Saler, *Gilded Virgin,* 1750

Opposite, main picture J.-L. David (1748–1825), *The Coronation of Napoleon*

Inset top Coronation of Frederick IV of Germany as Holy Roman Emperor in 1452 (detail), by anonymous Flemish master

Inset bottom Design by Vivienne Westwood, 1986/87

HATS OFF!

*Hat honour is as old as hats themselves. Doffing the hat is a sign of respect and even humility, though, as a picture of George V and the Prince of Wales shows (*opposite bottom right*), it is also the way of returning those things. Whether it is a king acknowledging the applause of the crowd or a man removing his hat when meeting a lady, the gesture is a gracious and frequently elegant one. In the 19th century it was a matter that preoccupied many men-about-town. Newspapers and periodicals gave advice on the latest mores of fashion and how they affected the speed of the doffing. The gesture sufficiently fascinated the photographer Eadweard Muybridge to appear as a sequence in his pioneer work of 1887.*

*The cry 'Hip, hip, hooray!' has always been associated with the removal of the hat, which is frequently thrown into the air on the final note. It is especially useful as a way of rousing feelings and lifting spirits and is therefore popular with politicians and the military. The Scots Fusiliers (*opposite top*) are cheering the Queen on the eve of their departure for the Crimean War in 1859.*

Top Parade of Scots Fusilier Guards
outside Buckingham Palace before
departure to the Crimea, 2 March 1859

Above George V and the Prince of Wales,
1930s

Left Loyal subjects greeting the Emperor
Franz Joseph, *c.* 1900

39

HOODS

The hood is a classic shape that has hardly changed over the centuries. It is designed either to frame the face or to shroud it. The architectural shape worn in the late 15th century by Lady Margaret Beaufort, Countess of Richmond (above), is echoed more softly but remarkably similarly by the hood worn today by women in Southern India (above right). Again, there is little difference in line between the hood worn by women in the Pyrenees in the 19th century (opposite left) and Christian Lacroix's overscale and superbly confident version for Jean Patou in 1986 (opposite).

Whether in stiffly starched linen or soft cotton flatteringly edged with beads, in strong cloth or finely woven straw, hoods outline and frame the face more eloquently than any other headwear. For this reason alone it is surprising that they have been revived so rarely in the 20th century. In a sense, their role has been taken over by the headscarf, though it has little of their flattery or charm.

Top left Anonymous, *Lady Margaret Beaufort* (Countess of Richmond), late 15th century

Above South Indian woman wearing headdress

Opposite top left Detail from a 19th-century popular print from the Pyrenees

Opposite, main picture Christian Lacroix for Jean Patou, 1986

Right Maquis of the Haute Loire, France,
World War II

Below Revolving series of portraits of
Che Guevara, Havana, Cuba

Opposite Beret of Guardian Angel in the
Paris metro, 1989

THE BERET: UNDERCOVER AND UNDERGROUND

In World War II the Basque beret was used by the French Resistance Movement, the Maquis (top left). It was an ambiguous choice of headgear. Though it has contemporary military associations – often with the suggestion of 'undress' uniform or covert operations – the beret was then the most common French headwear, a fact which enabled the Maquis to wear it without necessarily exciting suspicion.

Che Guevara, the hero of the Cuban revolution, helped to make the beret a worldwide symbol of the revolutionary guerrilla fighter. It is used today by the Guardian Angels, the vigilante group who patrol the subways and metros of some of the world's capital cities. The red beret shown above is worn by one of the Guardian Angels of Paris.

Left Dervish cap with inscription, Persia, *c.* 1850

Below Nemrut Dagh, Turkey

Opposite left Simone Martini, detail showing a courtier from the fresco of *The Investiture of St Martin as a Knight*, Chapel of St Martin at Assisi, *c.* 1320

Opposite right David Shilling, 1980s

THE SUGAR-LOAF HAT

The cone-shaped 'sugar-loaf' hat has been found in most civilizations at one time or another. The Dervish cap from Persia (opposite top) and the hat shown on the enormous stone head amid the ruins of the Mausoleum of Antiochus I in the Euphrates Valley are imposing in both height and scale. But this particular shape also has a practical advantage: in hot climates it helps to keep the head cool by trapping air inside the cone.

The 14th-century Italian courtier (left) uses his hat to give him height and stature. David Shilling's late 1980s creation (below), with its demure lace decoration, has more in common with the 18th-century mob cap.

Top left Vizier's turban on gravestone, Turkey, 18th century

Top right Detail from Iranian copper disc, *c.* 1600

Above left Schoolteacher, Jaipur, India

Above right Georges de la Tour (1593–1652), *The Card Cheater* (detail)

Opposite Jean-Paul Gaultier, 1988

THE TIMELESS TURBAN

The softly folded turban makes a shape as elegant as it is practical. It is also a shape that has endured for many centuries and has been adapted across many cultures with hardly any alteration. The turban shown on the 17th-century engraved metal disc from Iran (opposite top right) is clearly the same article as that worn by the modern Indian schoolteacher (opposite below left), whose own version echoes the turban carved on a vizier's gravestone in 18th-century Turkey. Similarly, the turban from Georges de la Tour's The Card Cheater (opposite below right) could be worn alongside Jean-Paul Gaultier's modern version (above) and look absolutely up to the minute. This form of headgear is one of the world's timeless designs.

As William Makepeace Thackeray wrote in his *Book of Snobs* in 1847, 'There is a great deal in the build and wearing of hats – a great deal more than at first meets the eye.' The history of the modern hat industry begins in the Middle Ages, although hats were known in the earliest civilizations. The basic raw materials for hatmaking are felt and straw. Legend has it that felt was discovered by St Clement (who was to become the fourth bishop of Rome), when he was a wandering monk. The story goes that he had a habit of stuffing his sandals with tow (flaxen fibre) to protect his feet from the roughness of the roads and he discovered that the combination of moisture and pressure from his feet matted the fibres together. After he became bishop he remembered his experience and set up groups of workers to develop the process of felting. Although without any factual basis, this legend persists: St Clement is the patron saint of felt hatmakers and St Clement's Day, 23 November, is the hatter's holiday.

In the hat industry, felt is made from animal hairs, usually the fur of rabbits, known as coney. But when the process first began in Europe, in the late Middle Ages, the fur normally used was beaver, and the best quality hats were always made from beaver hair. In fact, in the past, felt hats were known as 'beavers'. Beaver hats were prestigious objects, costly and precious – and worn only by the rich. By the end of the fourteenth century, they were being widely manufactured in the Low Countries: there were hatter communities in Louvain, Liège, Bruges, Brussels and Ghent. From there the trade spread to Spain, where felt hatmakers began to settle in towns evacuated by the Moors. Beavers were produced in Alicante, Seville, Cadiz and Malaga. Felt hat manufacturing reached London by the end of the fifteenth century and appeared in North America almost a century later.

Most beaver skins came from North America and the search for them was instrumental in the exploration of the northern reaches of the continent. Paradoxically, the furs most prized were secondhand skins that had been made into coats by the Indians and had been worn long enough for them to become greasy and dirty. These old skins, matted with sweat, felted most successfully. But there were never enough. Obtaining the skins was difficult and expensive and shipping them back to Europe was a slow and hazardous business. Supply could not meet demand.

The beaver remained at the top end of the market until the nineteenth century, when the hat of quality became the silk topper. Even in the early sixteenth century, the majority of 'beaver' hat manufacturers working in London were actually making rabbit-fur hats. These were produced sufficiently cheaply to be sold in considerable quantities and soon competed strongly with the old knitted cap industry which had

Modiste trimming a bonnet, *c.* 1840.

enjoyed a virtual monopoly in providing headwear for the masses. Eventually their popularity was so widespread that the makers of knitted caps panicked and petitioned the Crown for restrictive legislation to protect their industry. No fewer than five statutes were passed between 1511 and 1570 to protect the capmakers and, in the latter year, an edict was published commanding every male with a substantial income to wear a woollen cap on Sundays and Holy Days. But even such legislation could not stop the new fashion – the 'Flaunderish bever hat', as Chaucer had described it, had caught on.

Industrial improvements in the seventeenth and eighteenth centuries narrowed the gap between beaver and other furs and, by the nineteenth century, rabbit and hare were considered perfectly acceptable for all but the very best hats. These animals were trapped in their thousands. Furs from Australian rabbits were especially prized, as were those from Scotland, and the best hare was considered to come from Saxony. The Hudson's Bay Company exported the fur of a wide range of animals in an attempt to meet the European demand. Nutria and musquash were both acceptable substitutes for beaver at the better end of the market and the animals which provided them, the coypu and the muskrat, were trapped in vast numbers. Successful trappers became folk heroes. Kentucky-born Kit Carson, North America's most skilful trapper, was recognized and applauded wherever he went. But no matter how many American skins were exported, prices in Europe for real beaver did not drop. In an effort to produce a cheaper hat, experiments were carried out in Paris using the skins of rats, but these were unsuccessful. As the American poet Oliver Wendell Holmes wrote, 'Wear a good hat, the secret of your looks/Lies with the beaver in Canadian brooks.'

Strangely, although frontiersmen and mountain men in North America derived a considerable portion of their income from trapping beaver, they seldom wore beaver hats themselves. Presumably, the fur was simply too expensive. As protection from the bitter northern cold, they chose instead cheap fur, such as that of the bobcat,

Advertisement from the
Hatters' Gazette Diary, 1908.

coyote, fox and the ubiquitous raccoon. Often, they relied on blanketing caps, an all-embracing hood-type hat covering the neck down to the shoulders.

North America provided the fur; Europe helped pay for it by exporting finished hats to the growing number of American cities in the eighteenth century where life was still based on European standards and society was quite as formal as in Europe. However, the import–export equation was shattered when the Americans began to manufacture their own hats. The oldest hat centre in the United States is Danbury, in Connecticut, which was founded by eight families in 1684. It was there that Zadoc Benedict set up the first American hat factory in 1780. He employed one journeyman and two apprentices and they produced three hats per day. From this beginning, the U.S. felt hat industry grew and soon began to threaten Europe's hegemony. Not only could American manufacturers undercut imported hats – since they were free of the restrictive practices that proscribed European manufacturers in the eighteenth century – but they increasingly used slave labour to keep their costs down. As a result, they were able to export their hats at highly competitive rates. American manufactured hats were in great demand in Spain and the West Indies and sold well even in a traditional exporting market like England.

England had enjoyed an almost total monopoly in importing North American skins to Europe and had been able to control the flow to her own advantage. This changed during the eighteenth century as France received a greater proportion of skins, produced large numbers of high quality hats, and began to take over markets that had been previously controlled by Great Britain. By 1764 things had reached the point where the British manufacturers of beaver hats were seriously alarmed at the drop in sales to Europe (especially Spain and Portugal) and petitioned the government for tariffs to protect their livelihood. The petitioners calculated that France was costing them £50,000 a year in lost sales. A bill to protect them was passed in 1764.

Beaver hats were expensive, those of rabbit less so, but the cheapest material of all was straw. Although there are no references to straw hats in the Middle Ages, they certainly existed and, indeed, they were known in the ancient world. Clearly, they were so associated with peasants and agricultural workers that they appear rarely in literature or art. The earliest reference to a person of quality owning straw hats is in the list of possessions left by Sir John Fastoffe, who died in 1459. Straw hats for summer wear by people above the level of the labouring classes were almost certainly widespread across Europe by the seventeenth century. Light, comfortable and cheap, they were ideal country wear but they took a long time to become 'smart' – that is, suitable for wear on fashionable heads in towns. Even then, they were initially worn as a self-conscious gesture of sophisticated rusticity, rather like Marie Antoinette dressing up as a milkmaid. Straw hats were still country hats even when worn by eighteenth-century society beauties.

The straw hat worn by the fashionable lady was a far cry from those seen on the heads of women toiling in the fields. It was generally accepted that the best straw came from Italy and the most delicate hats were found in the district around Florence. In fact, Signia, a small town in Tuscany, was claimed in a British consular report of 1574 to be 'the original seat of the Italian straw industry' and Coryate mentions in his *Crudities*, published in 1611, that in Piedmont he had observed 'most delicate strawen hats, which both men and women use'. Such hats were exported to fashionable cities throughout Europe and it is undoubtedly Italian straws that the

The 18th-century writer, Mme d'Epinay, wearing the newly fashionable straw hat.

Swiss traveller De Saussure saw in London in 1727 when he noted that women 'even of the highest rank' were wearing small straw hats that he found vastly becoming, 'when they go out walking or make a visit.' If they were of the very highest quality, the hats will have come from Leghorn (Livorno) which was famous for producing the finest quality straw weave and the most beautifully worked hats. In fact, the word Leghorn entered the English language as an all-purpose word referring to the town, the material, the hat and the method of working the straw – as well as being the name of a well-known breed of chicken. Finer than anything produced elsewhere in Italy or Switzerland (her closest rival), Leghorn was the world's most expensive straw.

Italian and Swiss straws were not produced in such numbers that they could satisfy all the needs of other countries and, in England, high-grade straw was produced in Bedfordshire, Herefordshire and Buckinghamshire. At its height the industry employed more than 48,000 men, women and children but, by the end of the nineteenth century, the number had dropped to 30,000, despite encouragement at the highest level. The *Hatters' Gazette* of 1884 pointed out that several members of the royal family had taken to straw plaiting as a recreation, adding that 'Her Majesty takes an interest'. It sounds like desperate pleading for vested interests and almost certainly was. The idea that members of the royal household would deliberately engage in such a boring and repetitive pastime for any reason other than to give publicity to the workers in a hard-pressed industry was preposterous.

The dip in the English market was caused by the growing success of American straw hatters in supplying the needs of their home market. Having entered the field late, they caught up quickly and were soon producing hats as fine as most imported from Europe. The American industry was founded by a fourteen-year-old girl. In 1798 Betsey Metcalfe of Providence, Rhode Island, noticed an imported English straw bonnet in the window of a local haberdasher. As she could not afford to buy, she decided to copy it, using home-grown straw. Although completely inexperienced, Betsey produced a bonnet lined with pink silk that looked so professional that friends and neighbours gave her commissions. There had of course been indigenous straw hats before that date – Quaker girls in Pennsylvania had been making them for at least a century – but what Betsey Metcalfe did was to make a *fashionable* straw hat of the kind that American retailers had previously been obliged to import from Europe.

From this small beginning the American straw hat industry grew and flourished. But, as is the way of the fashionable world, imported hats then became even more attractive to the super-fashionable, who felt that a European chapeau must be superior to the home-grown variety. The American government, reacting just as the English had done a century or more earlier when threatened by France, imposed high duties on imported hats in the hope that Americans would turn away from them. The policy worked only at a certain level. The rich continued to desire exclusivity and were prepared to pay to achieve it. As the *Hatters' Gazette* commented in 1893, 'The belles of Saratoga and the White Mountains are always ready to give twice the price for an English straw in preference to the cheaper but really good productions of their own country – and this, too, in the face of absurdly heavy prohibitory rates.'

Despite the economic difficulties that periodically hit both the straw and the felt hat industries, profits were made and businesses flourished. But the workers rarely

Two of the stages in making a straw hat, 1878. *Top* Sorting the straw; *above* Sewing the plaited straw into hats by hand.

saw the financial benefits of their labour. Straw hat workers seem to have been more blatantly exploited than their counterparts in the felt industry. They came from the poorest section of the working class and were frequently sucked into the manufacturing world when very young. In the United States, child labour was part of the system of slavery but it existed just as widely in Europe and Great Britain. In the nineteenth century it was an abuse that was well known but, like many other industrial abuses in that uniquely hypocritical era, it was not acknowledged by those in power. In Luton, England, much of the exploitation was hidden by what appeared to be a philanthropic scheme for the children of workers. Hours in the industry were long; men and women usually worked until 9pm, except for Saturdays when the shift finished at 4pm. It was recognized that in the lead up to the summer, demand for straws would be so great that it would be necessary for workers to remain all night on Thursdays and Fridays so that hats would be ready for collection on Saturday mornings. In order that the workers' children could be looked after for some of the day at these and other times a system of 'dame schools', known as plait schools, evolved.

Initially set up as creches, the schools charged two pence per week. For that they were supposed to teach reading and writing but, in fact, most of the women in charge were illiterate. Conditions were appalling. Children were crowded in – as many as thirty in a room 12 foot square – and set to plaiting as young as three years old. The hours were long. The children normally plaited from 9am to 5pm and for those over seven there was an extra shift that frequently went on until 9pm. During all the time the children were in school they plaited, despite split fingers and mouths cut from sucking the straw to soften it. Their parents sold the products of this forced labour. Although such schools did not exist in Continental Europe, conditions there were little better. In Italy children began work as plaiters as a matter of course when they were still under ten.

For workers in the felt hat trade there were other hazards. Chief among them was the effect of inhaling fumes from the mercuric nitrate essential to the felting of animal furs, as well as the dust created by the felting process itself. Quite apart from the damage to the lungs, constant inhaling of the mercuric acid fumes affected the brain. The expression 'mad as a hatter' had a sound basis. Paralysis and loss of memory were followed by mental derangement and eventual death. Although the results were tragic, it was customary in the nineteenth century to make fun of those suffering from the disease. In the United States it was called the 'Danbury shakes' and throughout Europe sufferers were treated as drunkards rather than as men crippled by their work.

However, this attitude had some slight justification. Hat workers were notorious for quenching the thirst caused by the dust and fumes. Charles Booth in his *Life and Labour of the People in London*, published in 1896, pointed out that the hatmaking trade was 'full of strange customs, chiefly connected with drinking.' Drunkenness was common. So was rowdiness and a general belligerence that often led to disputes between workers and bosses. In the United States and Britain strikes were frequent throughout the nineteenth century, with lockouts, closed shops and all the unrest associated with a trade where many of the workers were itinerant and therefore badly paid. Hatters were often obliged to go from town to town looking for work. In England, the Hatters' Society of Great Britain and Ireland, commonly called the Fair Trade Union, issued white travelling cards to members who went 'on the

Lewis Carroll's 'Mad Hatter', from *Alice's Adventures in Wonderland*, 1865.

tramp' as proof of union membership and to enable them to draw a small benefit from local union branches until work could be found.

Conditions for milliners were hardly any better. In late nineteenth-century London, most milliners were resident, living above the shop or workroom where they were employed. For the employer this was a highly satisfactory arrangement: for a small extra outlay on food and beds he had a workforce at his command for as long as he required it. As with the straw hat industry, millinery hours were long. Few workers finished before 10pm and many went on beyond midnight. The only free day was Sunday, when the milliner was usually evicted from her room and sent out to fend for herself for the day, regardless of the weather, and with no food provided. Sleeping accommodation and working conditions were both appallingly crowded. Lit by weak gaslight that emitted dangerous fumes, and inadequately heated, the workrooms were crammed and fetid. Salaries were even lower than those for shop assistants. The conditions in London were not unique: in Paris, midinettes were fed so meagrely that fainting and exhaustion-induced illnesses were common. In human terms, the cost of hats for men and women in the nineteenth century was simply too high.

The world's first truly famous hatter was called Richard Sharp. Born in 1759 in Newfoundland, the son of a British army officer, he had made his fortune in hatting by the age of forty-six. He was renowned for the lavish hospitality he dispensed both at his Park Lane house and at his country retreat near Dorking in Surrey, where he entertained Coleridge, Wordsworth, Sydney Smith and Burke. In the 1790s he became involved in a movement for parliamentary reform known as 'The Friends of the People' and in 1804 was elected as a member of parliament for the pocket borough of Castle Rising in Norfolk. He remained in parliament for various seats until 1827. Known as 'Conversation' Sharp because of the excellence of his talk, he was a common sight in all the clubs and coffee houses of Regency England and was calculated to have more friends than any man in London. In love with literature, he published his own writings in *Letters and Essays in Prose and Verse* in 1834. Sharp died in 1835, leaving an estate worth £250,000.

The oldest hatter in the world is Lock's of St James's, London. The first Mr Lock – George James – was a merchant specializing in trade with Turkey who set up shop around 1676 in St James's Street. One of his neighbours was the hatter Charles Davis, whose clientele included the grand English landowning families such as the Bedfords and Devonshires. In 1747, George James Lock's grandson, James, became Davis's apprentice and in 1757 married his boss's daughter. Davis died a year later and Lock lost little time in changing the business name to his own. It has remained Lock's ever since.

Lock's is *the* British Establishment hatter. For over two hundred years many of the most important social, political and ecclesiastical heads have been fitted at 6 St James's Street. One nineteenth-century prime minister so trusted Lock's that he would stop his carriage in St James's, walk up to the door of the shop, shout 'Hat!' and leave. A new hat would be sent to him within the next few days. Bishop Wilberforce, son of William Wilberforce, wrote to the newly appointed Bishop of Lincoln:

> But I forgot to implore you to go to the right man for hats. Do get yours where my dear father got his – viz at Lock's in St James' Street, and if he asks you what

Lock & Co.,
St James's Street, London.

shape you prefer, say the same as that worn by your humble servant, which is the right one. I count on you to look charming.

Famed as the creator of the bowler, or derby, Lock's traded mainly with the military and landowning classes, to whom the firm were exceedingly gentle in the matter of prices and bills. They priced their hats so that they could survive the aristocratic habit of expecting very long credit. The price of a beaver remained one guinea for most of the eighteenth century, which allowed for the cost of credit. In the rare event of someone wishing to pay 'on the nose', the price was slightly reduced. The hatter's reward was the patronage of the great. At Garrick's funeral all ten of the pallbearers – including Earl Spencer, Viscount Palmerston and the Duke of Devonshire – were 'Lock's men'. Modern customers have included Charlie Chaplin, H.I.H. Prince Akihito of Japan and Queen Elizabeth II. At the time of Elizabeth's coronation in 1953, Lock's was commanded to create a hatband for the imperial state crown, which was too large for the Queen.

Another of London's famous hatters is Herbert Johnson, established in 1889 when Edward VII, then still Prince of Wales, promised his support to Johnson if he cared to set himself up in business. Johnson joined forces with Edward Glazier and opened at 45 New Bond Street. The royal connection continued when the Prince of Wales became king and granted the Royal Warrant to the firm. He was joined by the Tsar of Russia, the King of Norway and the King of Sweden. The royal connection continues today: Herbert Johnson are hatters by appointment to the Queen and the Prince of Wales.

Herbert Johnson hats are worn by virtually every regiment in the British army but, in addition, are frequently found in films. The showbusiness connection includes Indiana Jones's safari hat, which was designed on the Bond Street premises by Steven Spielberg and Harrison Ford; Jack Nicholson's hat in *Batman*; Rex Harrison's tweed trilby in *My Fair Lady*; and Inspector Clouseau's hat, which Peter Sellers always called his 'lucky hat'.

The most famous hatter in the United States was Genin of New York. Of French descent, from a family of hatmakers, his taste and skill were evident from the beginning, but what made him a household name was his brilliant flair for publicity. His shop was below Barnum's Museum on Broadway, which meant that everyone going to Wall Street and the business area of the city passed by. Genin became known to them all one hot day. He sent out hundreds of young men carrying handfuls of palm leaves, which they handed to every man on the street to use as a fan. On the handle of each was written 'Genin the Hatter'. As the evening rush uptown began, every merchant, banker, clerk and trader was talking about him, and many stopped off at his shop. His name was made. Keeping that name in the public mind was Genin's great skill. He pulled off his most daring coup in 1850, during the visit to the United States of Jenny Lind, the immensely popular 'Swedish Nightingale'. Demand for tickets for her concerts was so great that they were put up for auction. Genin purchased the best seat in the house for her first concert, paying one thousand dollars – a staggering amount at the time. His name, already famous, became legend when, on the night, his prominent seat remained vacant. All America was incredulous that a hatter could afford to be so arrogant.

The hatter with the strongest claim to the title 'Most Famous Hatmaker in the World' is the Italian family firm of Borsalino. Giuseppe Borsalino was born in Pecetto in northern Italy in 1834. He served his apprenticeship in Paris with Berteil, whose factory specialized in luxury beaver hats. In 1856 he returned to Italy and began to train a small team of workers. The first Borsalino hat was produced on 4 April 1857 in a courtyard in Via Schiavina in Pecetto. A year later, Borsalino was in proper premises in Via del Vescovado. From the beginning, the firm produced only a limited number of styles – for the first thirty years there were only six models. Although Borsalino started with only ten employees, by 1886 this number had increased to one hundred. Borsalino's heyday came in the early years of this century when he won the Grand Prix at the Paris Exhibition of 1900, then in Brussels in 1910, Turin a year later, and Paris again in 1931. By that time, his name was known worldwide as the maker of supremely stylish felt hats.

Although the best known, Borsalino is not the only Italian hatter with an international reputation. Giovanni Battista Gnecchi was a famous eighteenth-century hatter working in Melegnamo. He moved to Milan and won many prizes for his hats, which were known for their subtle colours. His two-colour hats of hare fur and silk were especially prized. Supported by the lawyer and writer Cesare Beccaria, he opened his factory in Santa Radegonda, Milan, in 1789. It was the first modern hat factory in Italy and produced about 5000 hats per year. They were greatly sought after by English gentlemen on the Grand Tour and it is highly likely that many a Macaroni minced around London in a Gnecchi hat, to the great distaste of his more soberly hatted compatriots.

Advertisements for the firm of Borsalino. *Right c.* 1900; *opposite* 1930.

HATMAKING

The skills involved in making a hat evolved in the 14th century and have hardly changed since. A workman familiar with the scenes depicted in L'Art de Faire des Chapeaux, published by M. Nollet in 1765 (above centre), would feel perfectly at home in a modern hat factory. Although the machinery might bewilder him, he would soon realize that the processes are still much as he knew them. For felt hats they include bowing (to remove and separate the fur); basoning (firming the fur by pressure); and blocking. The mercury used in curing felt was a common cause of poisoning which led to tremors, hallucinations and other psychotic symptoms. Hence the expression 'mad as a hatter'.

Top, *left to right* Beaver hatmaking, early 17th century; preparing the felt, rolling and heating, 1765; dyeing felt hats, 1765; the hatmakers' battery, 19th century

Far left below A blocking press for straw hats

Left below Proofing the felt body

Right Boon and Lane, Luton, England, 1991

STRAW HATS

Few items of clothing can successfully make the transfer from peasant's head to couturier's catwalk. The straw hat does so more successfully than most. The reason lies in its simplicity. Despite the great technical advances made in most areas of clothing in the 20th century, straw hats are still constructed in much the same way as they have always been. The peasant in Hugo van der Goes' 15th-century painting (right) would immediately recognize Hubert de Givenchy's elegant straw hat (opposite) as the same article as the one he holds in his hand. In fact, they could be exchanged and the difference would hardly be noticed. It is rare for the material of an item of clothing to determine shape as completely as straw does. It imposes its own discipline on the hatmaker. This is what gives straw hats their timeless quality. Their appeal is eternal — a modern woman could pick up any of the creations being made in 19th-century Dunstable (below) and wear it with pleasure today.

Left Hugo van der Goes (*c.* 1440–82), detail of the Portinari Altarpiece, Adoration of the Shepherds

Below Givenchy, haute couture, Summer 1990

Opposite below Straw hatmaking, Dunstable, England, early 19th century

Below left Straw bonnet from *Gallery of Fashion*, 1796

In the 19th and early 20th centuries, no man who considered himself a person of stature – quite apart from being a gentleman – went to work without a hat. It was part of the uniform of male power and superiority, whether the male was head of a bank or merely a humble 'teller'. Vast quantities of hats – felts, straws and silks in a remarkable variety of shapes and stylistic variations – were produced annually to fulfil an unending demand.

As both the hatters' trade and the requirements of customers grew more sophisticated in the middle years of the 19th century, it became apparent that traditional, rule-of-thumb means of measuring were simply not precise enough to take into account the myriad variations in individual heads. Hats made on a block of a uniform shape could not be expected to fit everybody. This problem was addressed by a French hatter, M. Maillard, who in 1843 patented an instrument called the conformateur, which could take an extremely precise head measurement.

But such precision was reserved for the bespoke end of the trade. Ready made hats were pushed out into the market with fewer refinements. Then, as now, a good hat could not be produced cheaply, but even the mass-produced working man's 'tile' was made to last and give value for money.

Right Using the conformateur, Bates Hatters, London, 1910s

Far right below Plaster moulds for hat blocks, Boon and Lane, Luton, England, 1991

Right below Boaters for an unusually hot summer, Luton, England, 1930s

HATS FOR GENTLEMEN

The earliest cars were usually open vehicles, so ladies in large, feather-laden picture hats or extravagantly scaled tulle toques could experience at one and the same time both the latest fashion and the latest transport. But such a happy amalgam did not last. The modern motor car killed for ever the more extreme examples of the milliner's skills. Yet the love affair between fashion and the machine continued well into the 1920s, when the concept of streamlining became central to creativity. The cloche hat in Tamara Lempicka's Autoportrait (opposite top) is based on a racing driver's helmet and is as sleek as any of the cars and aeroplanes that were coming off assembly lines in increasing numbers at that time.

Certain cars have always stood for glamour. The Hispano-Souza, Daimler-Benz and Rolls Royce are the haute couture of automobiles; they were, and still are, cars to dress up to. An elegant woman wearing a model hat needs a glamorous car to add the final touch, just as early lady motorists did. Shiny and straight-edged, the motor car offers the perfect contrast to the softness of a beautiful hat.

If the hat has a veil, it provides yet another link with the early days of motoring. The unmetalled roads still in existence at the turn of the century meant that summer motorists ended up covered in dust. To overcome this problem women often wore enormously long and wide crepe-de-chine or chiffon veils. Pinned to their hats, they were wrapped around the head and face and tied in a bow under the chin. The favourite colours for veils were beige, cream and grey, all shades that helped to disguise the dust.

MILLINERY AND MOTORS

Far left Lady at the wheel, 1910

Centre Tamara Lempicka, *Autoportrait*, c. 1925

Below Advertisement for Opel, c. 1910

Bottom Frederick Fox, 1988

Opposite below Advertisement for Tuborg
Breweries Ltd, Copenhagen, 1905

THE BOWLER

Although essentially a comic shape, the bowler has long been the chief symbol of male power dressing. It was the hat of both the city gent and the man of affairs until well into the 20th century. But it can also represent the pathos of dented dignity, as Chaplin's battered bowler invariably does, no matter how jauntily he may cock it.

It is a paradox that such a no-nonsense practical hat – invented as a durable headcovering for ghillies and fieldworkers whose soft hats could not withstand the daily punishment of rural life – so frequently appears in dreams and the unconscious. Surrealists like René Magritte fully understood that a bowler could have an erotic as well as a sinister charge.

Opposite René Magritte, *The Masterpiece or the Mysteries of the Horizon*, 1955

Left Charlie Chaplin in *The Gold Rush*, 1925

Below Bowler, James Lock & Co., 1990

HAT FESTIVALS

The Easter Parade was a 19th-century American invention and has now largely disappeared. But the Easter bonnet is still very much part of the millinery scene and milliners everywhere rush to get their hats ready in time for them to be photographed for the newspapers as personifying 'The Spirit of Easter'. To win such publicity, an Easter bonnet must be witty and outrageously eye-catching. It does not need to be wearable.

In France, St Catherine is the patron saint of milliners, and unmarried women over the age of twenty-five who sew and make hats for couturiers or milliners are called Catherinettes. Once a year, on St Catherine's Day, 25 November, a party is held in their honour and the highlight of the occasion is the display of extravagant hats the women have made for themselves in their spare time. This tradition, dating from the 19th century, has been kept alive by couturiers of the stature of Jeanne Lanvin and Christian Lacroix.

Opposite top Jeanne Lanvin with her Catherinettes, 1945

Opposite below Christian Lacroix with his Catherinettes, 1991

Top Carlos Lewis with a model wearing one of his Easter hats, Easter 1991

Right Aage Thaarup, 'The Birth of an Easter Bonnet', 1940

THE
MAD HATTERS'
TEA PARTY

*A triumvirate of talent: Philip
Treacy, Nicholas Oakwell, Stephen
Jones. Three of London's most
talked about milliners hold their own
Mad Hatters' tea party wearing the
styles that exemplify their different
talents. Lewis Carroll would surely
have approved of the Alice in
Wonderland spirit they all reveal.*

    *Treacy's elongated bowler sits on
his head rather like a missile about
to be launched; Oakwell's feathered
extravaganza could grace the head
of any duchess in an Oscar Wilde
play and Jones's witty cross between
a turban and a top hat would bring
the house down were it worn by a
circus clown. All three hats
exemplify the 'fou' of millinery that
keeps people talking about creations
and creators just as much now as in
any period of fashion since the days
of Rose Bertin and the court of
Versailles.*

    *Although London-based, these
milliners enjoy international
reputations and their designs are in
demand by the world's top
couturiers. Their hats are
photographed for the glossiest
magazines and are even worn by
women in the cold and realistic light
of day. The realism comes when the
bill is to be paid. Fantasy on this
level does not come cheap – but then,
no high fashion ever has.*

Left to right Philip Treacy, Nicholas
Oakwell, Stephen Jones, 1991

THE PARTY

*S*tage and vaudeville entertainers have always worked within a limited number of hat styles. The boater, the bowler and the topper have been their stock-in-trade for two hundred years. Symbolic women's hats have appeared less often, though in music hall and pantomime comic working-class women, frequently played by men, have often been shown wearing a black poke bonnet, slightly the worse for wear, or a cheap straw hat with a bedraggled feather. Symbolism in women's hats came fully into its own only with the cinema goddesses of the 1920s and 1930s.

The earliest vaudeville hat acts were known as 'chapeaugraphy'. These involved a single performer with one prop – a large felt hat brim with a hole in the middle instead of a crown. Through this the performer pushed his head. Then, working at lightning speed, he twisted the brim into a variety of different shapes resembling current hat styles. Changing his expression to suit each new shape, the chapeaugraphist was able to portray dozens of different characters – male and female, haughty and abject – in quick succession. The whole act rarely lasted more than ten minutes, but a good performer could create as many as fifty different characters, each with an appropriate hat.

Chapeaugraphy was originally conceived in the 1750s by the French mime artist Tabarin but, despite its popularity at the time, it died with him and was not revived for more than one hundred years. In 1870 Monsieur Fusier, a Parisian vaudeville star, reintroduced the skill to instant acclaim. His act, which included dialogue, presented fifteen character portraits created from his black felt brim. The international tours of rival French performer Felicien Trewey made chapeaugraphy a craze in the 1900s. Billed as 'Many Faces under a Hat' or 'Hats Make the Man', chapeaugraphy not only played to packed theatres – it was usually the act that opened the second half of the show – but also became a popular form of home entertainment.

The success of chapeaugraphy resides in the fact that until World War II hat culture was a part of everyday life. Because everyone wore a hat, certain types of people became linked with particular styles. This still happens, of course, with other items of clothing: we all have a preconceived idea of the personality of the duffle-coated sandal-wearer, or the man in the Brooks Brothers shirt. In the past hats carried very precise and powerful semiotic messages and these were what music-hall comedians built on. The battered topper symbolized pretensions to gentility – or the

'The Party', 19th-century book illustration.

self-indulgence that caused a man 'to come down in the world'. The poke bonnet suggested narrow-minded bigotry, moral rectitude or pride. In theatre as in life, hats proclaimed the man and the woman.

Nineteenth-century theatre reviews teem with references to hats. A critic writing in the *Hatters' Gazette* in 1897 reflected on the 'wonderful share which hats possess in the amusement and gratification of the public', and noted that it is

> only the portrayer of swelldom who treats his hat in a proper and dignified manner. He is, as a rule, careful to wear a smooth glossy tile which is in harmony with the character he is depicting, but occasionally some of this latter class discard all idea of propriety and make a crush opera-hat serve their every purpose, whether they be attired in a faultless dress suit or a fashionable morning costume. Negro delineators and duettists, however, often depend upon the shape or posture of the hat they wear to raise a laugh, in which aim they are seldom unsuccessful. Hats without crowns or deprived of brims, or perforated from top to bottom, when manipulated in a comical way, can evoke many a shout of merriment from the gaping crowd that flocks to a music hall or concert room . . . Clever tricks, too, that afford no little satisfaction are done with conical-shaped hats by many an adroit clown or expert gymnast. They are twisted about on sticks and umbrellas, thrown up towards the roof to alight skilfully on the head, and sent spinning through the air a distance of twenty or thirty yards to be caught again by some dexterous accomplice at the further end of the building.

Hat used by the celebrated 19th-century French conjuror Robert-Houdin.

Magicians have often used hats as a central prop in their act. The first man to produce a rabbit from a hat was Louis Comte, a court entertainer in France who performed the trick in 1814 and instantly added a new skill to the repertoire. The hat trick became standard fare and by the 1830s had become the core of many popular acts. It retained its popularity throughout the nineteenth century, and those who excelled at it became rich men. Joseph Hartz, born in Liverpool in 1836, performed the hat trick so successfully around the world that he was awarded medals by the kings of Spain, Denmark and Greece as well as by the President of Mexico.

Of course, it was not just rabbits that were produced from hats. Jacques Talon, who performed under the name Philippe in the early 1800s, conjured endless flowers out of his. Ludwig Dobler, performing at around the same time, in Vienna, always finished his act by trampling and crushing his hat and then coaxing from its ruins small bouquets of flowers which he threw to the ladies in the audience. Milliners loved him and regularly named hats after him. Sleight of hand with coins and top hats made T. Nelson Downs one of America's top vaudeville stars, along with Karl Germain, whose act consisted of catching coins in a hat borrowed from the audience and changing them into candy, which was then distributed by his assistant. He ended his act by first cooking an omelette in a top hat and then producing from the same hat a three-course dinner, complete with cutlery and tablecloth. There appeared to be no limit to what could come out of a hat. John Henry Anderson, the Scottish music-hall star, drew 'hot' puddings from his; Cecil Lyle in London, billed as the Magical Milliner, produced women's hats from his and the American performer Howard Thurston used an outsize hat out of which popped scantily dressed chorus girls.

But top hats had other uses. Before becoming a cinema actor, W. C. Fields was a famous top hat juggler in vaudeville and in musical revues on Broadway. Billed as

Detail from a trade card used by the milliner Charlotte Truchot, Paris, 1919.

'The Juggler Tramp' because he always wore a battered and torn topper, his finest act was 'The Change Hat Trick', which he performed with his top hat, a cigar and a clothes brush. As a contemporary described it, 'He balanced the hat on one lifted foot and the cigar in his mouth and, at the same time, tossed the brush over his head and into his back pocket.'

If the hat entertained on stage, it frequently irritated in the auditorium. As the nineteenth century came to its end, women's hats grew larger. By the beginning of the twentieth century they were of unprecedented height and width, laden with decorations and heavy with veils. In wearing hats of such magnitude, women were following the lead of the great actresses of the day, all of whom favoured extravagant headwear both on and off stage. Theatrical costume at the time was designed on a grand scale and hats followed suit. Exotic birds and whipped-cream concoctions of tulle sparkled with semi-precious stones; rich velvets were speared with bejewelled hatpins of a size that ensured that their magnificence could be picked up throughout the theatre, and especially in the gods, where actresses knew that their most fanatical admirers would be sitting. Such grandeur on stage was mirrored in the auditorium, to the great irritation of those who found themselves sitting behind these magnificent confections. A spate of critical letters and satirical verses commented on the phenomenon. Walter Buell's poem 'It Was the Hat' so exactly reflected a common experience that it became popular with theatregoers far beyond his native Australia:

> I sat behind her at the play
> (They say it was *Othello*)
> But who appeared, and how 'twas done –
> Well, ask some other fellow.

75

I heard a sweet, entreating voice,
A stifled shriek and groan, a
Silence that, I take it, marked
The Death of Desdemona

And this was all; I simply write
These lines as a reminder
To someone that I lost the play
Because I sat behind her.

A writer in the *Buffalo Express* commented, 'Everybody is saying that the Gainsborough hat "must go". Confound it, that's just what it does do – to all the shows'. An article in a weekly paper published in 1887 referred to 'the awful female hat' and described it as crushing the face with 'an enormous tower of straw or felt, trimmed with bows and feathers and things that waggle and flowers and birds and I know not what at all'. This description, which brings the millinery of the time more alive than most fashion commentaries do, notes that some of these hats were as high as twenty inches and 'are just the thing that Job ought to have been asked to sit behind at the theatre to give his patience a *real* trial'.

By 1892 the problem had become so serious that the manager of the Grand Opera House in Minneapolis was sued by a customer who claimed that although his view had been entirely blocked by the enormous hats of the two ladies in front of him the attendant had refused to change his seat and the manager had denied him a refund. Managers were indeed in a quandary. They needed the patronage of the *bon ton*, but could not allow the extreme fashions favoured by the latter to frighten off other customers. In an attempt at a compromise, Tom Davies, who ran the Queen's Theatre in London, instituted a new system in 1908 whereby large hats were banned at matinees. Tickets included a warning that attendants would insist on hats being removed once ladies were seated. As a chivalrous gesture, David allowed women over fifty to keep their heads covered provided they wore 'close-fitting bonnets'. Since evening performances encouraged flamboyant dressing on both sides of the footlights, complaints at such performances were ignored, as a 'suitable alternative has been provided'.

Hats in film have regularly been used to create a character and many stars became identified with a particular style. But the hat that has proved to be the greatest gift to actors is the bowler. Film makers never saw it as a 'toff's' hat, like the top hat, but, reflecting real life, used it to symbolize the boss class at only one or two removes from the blue-collar worker. On the head of Charlie Chaplin, it represented the pathetic vulnerability of the man whose dignity derives from his hat. Coupled with his shabby suit, crooked walking stick and absurdly 'cocky' walk, Chaplin's bowler signalled to cinema audiences that here was an embattled little man using his hat to give him solidity and importance. The fact that both hat and man were always being knocked off their pedestals made the character irresistible.

Marie Lloyd wore a battered hat symbolizing faded grandeur when she sang her famous Cockney song, 'I'm One of the Ruins that Cromwell Knocked about a Bit' in London's music halls, but female hats in films were used almost exclusively to suggest glamour. During the 1930s and 1940s, costume designers created hats for the screen goddesses that were designed more to express personalities than to fit the needs of the plot. Loretta Young in her elegant cartwheels, Garbo in her slouch felt cloche, Dietrich in shiny black feathers and half-veils became icons of elegance and sophistication. In the days when Hollywood viewed extravagance almost as an act of faith, designers had a field day with hats. Adrian, Walter Plunkett and Travis Banton created, on and off screen, millinery that was the essence of chic and elegance. As soon as the films were distributed the styles were copied by mass manufacturers. In prestigious productions, the star's personal milliner — Lilly Daché, Hattie Carnegie or Sally Victor — would be called in to design her hats. These were then frequently copied and modified for the designer's 'model' range for the season. John Frederics, who created Garbo's slouch hat, fathered a fashion that ran for more than ten years. Costume dramas like *Forever Amber* and *Du Barry Was a Lady* were the excuse for outrageously extravagant hats and hairstyles that often had little to do with historical verisimilitude and everything to do with making a memorable impression.

In using hats to define character, film directors were merely making through a twentieth-century medium a statement which writers and poets had been making for a long time. W. C. Fields's 'rather tipsy topper' exemplified Oliver Wendell Holmes's comment: 'Shabby gentility has nothing so characteristic as its hat. There is always an unnatural calmness about its nap and an unwelcome gloss suggestive of a wet brush.' In 'The Adventure of the Blue Carbuncle', Conan Doyle shows Sherlock Holmes solving a mystery by drawing certain conclusions from 'a very seedy and disreputable hard hat, much the worse for wear, and cracked in several places'. Begging Watson to look upon it not 'as a battered billycock but as an intellectual problem', Holmes proceeds to deduce the character of its owner from the hat's state and style. 'This hat', he says, with the total assurance that always stunned Watson, 'is three years old. These flat brims curled at the edge came in then. It is a hat of the very best quality. Look at the band of ribbed silk and the excellent lining.' Watson, who has seen nothing but 'a very ordinary black hat of the usual round shape', is suitably impressed. Holmes goes on to prove that the man's wife no longer loves him, as the hat has not been brushed for weeks; that his house is without gas light, from the tallow stains on the hat; and that he perspires freely — for which 'proof positive' are the marks of moisture on the inside. After such masterly deduction, the actual solution of the crime is child's play.

The style of hat favoured by Arthur Conan Doyle himself was not sufficiently remarkable to cause comment by his contemporaries so it is unlikely to have been as distinctive as Holmes's deerstalker. Conan Doyle presumably chose this style for his hero in order to signify a controlled eccentricity — or, at least, an oblique and original attitude to life. Essentially a country sportsman's style, it suggests that the man who wears such a hat in town as well as in the country can be relied upon to get beneath the surface and discover the truth. In Victorian England, the deerstalker — the hat of the hunter — was an ideally symbolic 'prop' for someone whose life was dedicated to seeking out wrongdoers and bringing them to book.

Writers, like painters, are often negligent of their appearance. In some cases, the neglect reflects a genuine disregard for the rules of society; in others, it is a carefully calculated pose meant to advertise a mind beyond thoughts of trivial dress conventions. Either way, eccentric dress has always been a way of attracting publicity. A New York newspaper described Walt Whitman's hat as a 'knockabout serving as hat, fan and sometimes even a tablecloth. He has been known to eat his dinner out of its capacious crown.' Robert Louis Stevenson was notorious for wearing headgear that 'might once have been a hat'. Stevenson's hats were in fact so old and unsuitable for London that even his biographer, J. A. Steuart, referred to his battered straw hat as something 'his grandfather must have worn and laid aside because it was out of date'.

Stevenson was one of the nineteenth-century's true eccentrics, but other writers were perfectly happy to strike a pose: tiny Max Beerbohm wore an exceptionally tall hat in order to give him height. G. K. Chesterton was regularly seen in the dining room of Paddington Station in 'a black sombrero and an enormous cloak, a cup of tea in one hand and a glass of port in the other'. W. S. Gilbert was rarely seen in anything other than a light grey suit and white topper.

Nineteenth-century actors were keener to be considered 'raffish' than their modern equivalents, which explains why Henry Irving was a famous sight in London wearing his 'widewake perched jauntily on one side and his hair falling almost over his shoulders', although by 1912 Douglas Fairbanks stood out in Piccadilly as the only man formal enough to be wearing a top hat and tailcoat. Eugène Labiche, whose play *An Italian Straw Hat* was filmed by René Clair in 1927, was renowned in Paris for the elegance of his hats – and the astronomic proportions of his hatter's bills. In one of his plays, he contrived a scene in which a character was to be recognized by his stolen hat. In an attempt to have his hat bill written off, Labiche suggested to his hatter that one of the actors would pick up the stolen hat and read the hatter's name as the label. This was agreed, but, as luck would have it, the actor was in similar debt to his own hatter and had made him exactly the same promise.

There is an element of show in the headdress of sportsmen, especially those whose sport presupposes an audience. But the overriding consideration for all sportsmen is that their hats and caps should give them protection. Sports hats are usually the ad hoc answer to a specific and even localized problem. Most players have a streak of fanaticism that means that they will not abandon a game or leave a match unfinished simply because of a change in the weather. Hats have been integral to many sports for this very reason, growing up informally with the game and often becoming uniform only after many years. Although they may assume social and class significance once a game is fully developed, sporting hats usually begin as essentially practical items. It is easy to see why. Most games were originally impromptu activities, played during breaks from work or in leisure hours. Players therefore wore their ordinary working or everyday clothing. Cricket, for example, was played for over a century without a formal cricket cap. Those who needed a headcovering wore the straw hats that gave them protection against the sun as they worked in the fields. In fact, the main purpose of a sports hat is to protect the eyes from the sun, which is why so many sports – from horse racing to baseball – evolved a hat or cap with a visor or peak.

However, there were exceptions. No sun visor or peak was used in early versions of the golfer's hat, probably because the modern game originated in Scotland. Until well into the nineteenth century the golfer's cap was little more than a beret or tam-o'-shanter. Knitted or woven, it was worn more for warmth and protection from the wind than against the sun and had more in common with the stalker's tweed cap than with any other form of sports headwear. It was this basic shape that was developed in

Selection of hats from the Jordan, Marsh and Company catalogue, 1891.

Hunting cap

Double ender

Bicycle cap

Baseball cap

Lady's riding jockey-cap

the twentieth century. Although many nineteenth-century golfers wore hard hats on the links, the tweed cap eventually became standard golfing wear. Large and commodious by the 1920s, it was worn by all golfers from the Prince of Wales down. In the latter part of the twentieth century, golf has, like most sport in the television era, become much more aggressively marketed than in the past and the professional golfer's hat reflects this by often looking more like a baseball cap than a traditional golfer's cloth cap.

There is little in the game of golf that makes a cap necessary for safety. Jockey caps, by contrast, are essential protective headwear. They must combine lightness with toughness and for that reason the earliest caps were made of felt stiffened with gum arabic. They had a wide, visor-type peak, to protect the eyes from the mud thrown up by the horses in front, and a ribbon tie at the back which could be adjusted to ensure a firm fit. Caps were originally black and continued to be so even after 1762, when the Duke of Cumberland instituted National Jockey Club colours for British racing. By 1887, when all colours had to be registered, British caps were made in the owner's colours, as were the jockey's silk shirts. The stiffened hat – bowler or topper, according to the occasion – became standard riding wear for hacking or hunting, although polo players in the Bois de Boulogne at the turn of the century chose pillbox hats tied under the chin.

The cricket cap did not become an essential item of kit for serious players – amateur or professional – until the late nineteenth century. Earlier in the century players were still wearing a variety of styles. Cricketers at Princeton and Yale in the

English cricket team on board ship at Liverpool, before leaving for the United States, 1859.

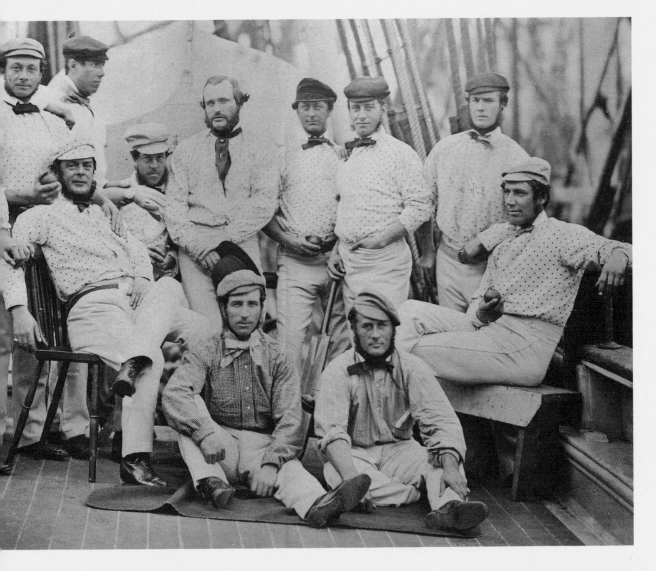

79

late 1870s wore knitted skullcaps for college matches. In England, too, this bowl-shaped hat was popular throughout the nineteenth century though many cricketers chose to continue the late eighteenth-century practice of wearing a high hat for the game, a choice that may have been influenced by a cricket club ruling of 1820 that 'if any person stops the ball with his hat the ball is considered dead'.

The hat was clearly an article of some talismanic importance in nineteenth-century cricket, as it was in daily life, which presumably explains why it was the item chosen for the award to H. Stephenson in Sheffield in 1858 for taking three wickets with consecutive balls – the first recorded 'hat trick'. Although the style of hat in question is unknown, one feels that only a hard hat, preferably a topper, would have sufficient dignity for the occasion. By 1888, W. G. Grace's classic book, *Cricket*, which did so much to codify and tidy up the game, recommended a cap instead of a hat for players. It was the beginning of a process that was to turn the cricket cap into a ritualistic object to which much cricketing superstition attached itself, not least the idea that a man's cap brought him luck. The *Sydney Morning Herald* described how the Australian cricketer 'Plum' Warner so revered his cap – 'a thoroughly foul-looking old rag of a thing' – that he would not walk out on to a pitch without it.

The situation was much the same in baseball. The baseball cap was originally brimless. The eight-piece peaked version was popularized during the Depression by Babe Ruth, who played for the New York Yankees. With its deep sun visor which, for outfielders, was often equipped with sunglasses, the baseball cap was so essential an item of equipment for the game that a mythology built up around it. Its lettering and trimmings identified the team. It was inevitable that supporters would want to wear their team's cap to proclaim their support and baseball caps became an item of daily wear in North America during the 1920s, when baseball players were exalted to superstar status. Champions such as Ruth, whose record for home-run hitting was never equalled, made baseball the national game and the baseball cap the classless headgear of a nation dedicated to egalitarianism. At a time when poverty was widespread and immigrants were searching for something to make them feel that they belonged to their new nation, the baseball cap – cheap, totemic and exclusively American – proved to be the perfect unifying headwear.

Opposite French advertisement for 'Royal Derby' golf hat, *c.* 1930; *below* Victorian lady golfer in hat with feather trim.

Gas station attendants, table-wipers in the diner, agricultural workers and truck drivers all adopted the baseball cap as the ideal working hat and it became the symbol of middle-American mundaneness, immortalized in Norman Rockwell's covers for the *Saturday Evening Post*. There it could have remained. But in the social revolution that hit the United States in the 1960s, the baseball cap began to take on a different significance. It became the hat of the radical white college boy at variance with his consumer-orientated parents, as well as the defiant cap of the newly urbanized poor blacks and Hispanic immigrants who had few skills and fewer hopes in the inner cities of the nation. The baseball hat assumed a new political dimension. Yet, despite the fact that Rick Nielson, the lead guitarist of Cheap Trick, wore a baseball cap in the late 1970s, it was not until rap and hip hop in the 1980s that it became the hat of the new music. As such, it achieved enormous popularity worldwide and became the more or less 'official' headwear of hip hop when worn with the brim to the side or the back. But, whether worn by Public Enemy or by Bruce Springsteen, baseball caps make a statement about the individual and his attitude to society and have become for many young people a badge of defiance and a symbol of alienation from a culture they are unable to escape.

BOATERS

Opposite top John Singer Sargent, *Mr and Mrs Isaac Newton Phelps Stokes* (detail), 1897

Opposite At rest on the river, 1888

Above Givenchy, haute couture, A/W 1990/91

Above right Poster by Charles Kiefer, 1936

*Since its invention in the 1880s, the boater has been a jaunty, cheeky upstart of a style, never to be taken too seriously. It was the headwear of the young when en fête in summer and was worn by demure young ladies and mashers alike. The manner of wearing it was all-important. The stolid lady on the river (*opposite*) proclaims her lack of style by wearing hers in such an uncompromising and unimaginative way: fashion demanded a rakish angle. Just how far forward and how far to the side was a matter of some debate at the turn of the century. When, in the 1920s, Maurice Chevalier made the boater his signature hat he wore it at an angle so stylishly raffish that, like his accent, jutting lower lip and fabulous smile, it became an essential part of his legendary success in Hollywood in the following decade.*

Sadly, men have now abandoned the boater along with most other hat styles, but it still makes the occasional pert appearance on the catwalk as a style for women.

TENNIS
HEADGEAR

Time was when the cry, 'Anyone for tennis?', was the invitation to a refined and peaceable activity suitable for ladies on long hot summer afternoons. The mood of those times is perfectly caught by the early 1900s poster (far left) and the turn-of-the-century calendar showing a gentleman and his partner dressed for a game clearly not meant to be too energetic (left). By the 1920s, the pace had increased and competition was taken seriously by amateur and professional alike, but it was not until relatively

recently that tennis became a highly combative and aggressive game, played at enormous speed by women as well as men. Hats no longer feature in such a fast and furious world. Their place has been taken by the far more functional headband.

Opposite top left Poster for musical comedy, *Skipping to the Light of the Moon*, 1900s

Opposite top right September, calendar published in Boston, 1895

Opposite below left Helen Wills, Carlton Club, Cannes, 1926

Opposite below right Soviet Union, 1928

Above André Agassi, Wimbledon, 1991

Left Pat Cash, Wimbledon, 1987

HATS
THAT SWING

*Ask any jazz musician why he wears a hat
and he will tell you that it gives him that
sense of style essential if he is to 'swing'.
Many of the 'greats', from Fats Waller to
Boy George, have worn trademark hats to
set the mood for the performance to come.
Even if the audience did not know what
sort of song to expect from Burning Spear
(centre top), his hat would immediately
make it clear, just as Don Williams's
would (centre bottom).*

*It is not just at the pop concert or on
the stage that hats so instantly set a mood.
In everyday life, we can judge people's
attitudes and opinions (as well, of course,
as their taste and income) the moment we
see their hat. The old slogan, 'If you want
to get ahead, get a hat' was undoubtedly
true, but a rider could also have been
added: 'If you want to hide your attitudes,
go bareheaded.'*

Clockwise from top left Boy George; Burning
Spear, 1990; Fats Waller (1904–43); John Lee
Hooker, 1984; Don Williams; Rikki Lee Jones

MOVIE GLAMOUR

The cinema's cliché glamour hat is the wide-brimmed Edwardian affair popularized by Cecil Beaton in My Fair Lady, *but it is not the only way in which screen goddesses have made their mark over the years. In fact, the more sophisticated the actress the smaller and simpler the hat has been. Dietrich rarely wore large hats; Garbo's androgynous beauty almost always looked its best in a small, face-framing style. The 'Brazilian Bombshell', Carmen Miranda, on the other hand, chose hats that would reflect the outrageous theatricality of her personality and made sure that they were piled as high as humanly possible with exotic fruit, flowers and vegetables that shimmered and shook as she danced.*

Clockwise from top left Marlene Dietrich; Theda Bara as Cleopatra, 1917; Carmen Miranda; Greta Garbo as Mata Hari, 1931; Audrey Hepburn in *My Fair Lady*, 1964

THE BASEBALL CAP

George Bernard Shaw described baseball as a combination of cricket, lawn tennis and Handel's Messiah, and it certainly does have a heroic element when played by men of the calibre of Babe Ruth, who reached the apex of his career in 1927 by hitting sixty home runs. Paul Gallico wrote of him, 'There has always been a magic about that gross, ugly, coarse, gargantuan figure of a man and everything he did', and surely the way he wore his cap was part of it. This same magic has been kept alive by other 'greats', such as Joe di Maggio, and the baseball hat is now firmly ensconced as the headwear of heroes.

It has a special appeal, too, for members of the entertainment world. When Elton John chose a sequined version for a concert at the Dodger Stadium in Los Angeles (right), he was making a witty comment on the fragility of the macho image which the baseball cap has always epitomized. British comedian Lenny Henry (below) followed Elton John's decorative lead but gave his hat an extra 'cool' dimension by wearing it back to front. Even controversial film directors like Spike Lee (far right) benefit from the confidence that the baseball cap gives. Although baseball is a quintessentially American game, it is almost as popular in Japan (opposite below), where more people play – and watch – than anywhere else outside the United States.

Right Elton John, Los Angeles, 1966

Centre Babe Ruth

Far right Spike Lee

Below Lenny Henry

Far right below Member of Tokyo University basketball team, 1968

PUTTING ON MY TOP HAT

'I'm puttin' on my top hat . . .', sang Fred Astaire at his most debonair, before demonstrating that a great dancer could still move immaculately even when wearing the hat least suited to rapid motion. Astaire knew that the top hat was a sign of quality on stage as much as in real life. In the days when most men aspired to being gentlemen, the top hat was the outward and visible sign that they had succeeded. But it was with white tie and tails for evening wear that the top hat truly came into its own.

The outfit is even more elegant on a woman, to whom it gives a mysteriously ambiguous allure. Many of the world's great actresses and entertainers have found the effect irresistible. The pioneer work of Vesta Tilley, who wore top hat and tails for her early music-hall acts, was continued by the French actress Réjane, and later by the movie star Mary Pickford, who knew that the outfit would add an extra piquancy to her innocent image. But it is Marlene Dietrich, the personification of the sophisticated woman, who has made top hat and tails her trademark. Although the top hat still reappears regularly on stage and screen, no one has ever worn it with quite her insouciant confidence.

Far left, top to bottom Marlene Dietrich, New York City, 1959; Mary Pickford in *Kiki*, 1931; Réjane (1857–1920)

Left Fred Astaire in *Top Hat*, 1935

Below Hat by Thierry Mugler, late 1980s

HATS FOR RIDING

The equestrienne has regularly featured in European and North American art and the most distinctive aspect of her dress has often been her headwear, chosen as frequently to impress as to afford protection. The early-15th-century lady depicted left wears a style fashionable at the time which is in no sense a riding hat in the modern meaning of the word. Later examples of headwear for riding women not only had an element of protection but were often adaptations of current men's hat styles.

Opposite top Gallery of Fashion, 1795

Main picture The month of May, Les Très Riches Heures du Duc de Berry, early 15th century

This page, top Auguste Renoir, The Amazons (detail), 1873

Above Riding hat by James Lock & Co., 1991

95

Hats express social attitudes and are as limited by convention as any other items of dress. There were always rules about when and how a hat might be worn and they were rules that had to be obeyed. When Philip Bosinney in *The Forsyte Saga* called on the aunts of his fiancée 'in a soft grey hat, not even a new one – a dusty thing with a shapeless crown', they and all the Forsyte family were alarmed by his unconventional attitude. By choosing a soft instead of a hard hat for such a formal visit, Bosinney showed himself to be unreliable, arrogant and far too unorthodox for their well-ordered world. To show their disapproval, they dubbed him 'The Buccaneer'. His hat told them that, for all his charm, he was a rogue.

John Galsworthy wrote *The Forsyte Saga* in 1906 – the Edwardian period, which saw the last great flowering of the hat for both sexes. In early twentieth-century England, hat lore was rigid, but it was equally as strong anywhere that Western dress was worn – from Tallahassee to Turin, Berlin to Brisbane. Hats for both sexes were part of the semiotics of power and all social classes abided by the rules governing their use. Only Bohemians, Romantics and Revolutionaries refused to kowtow – a refusal that was viewed with disapproval by the authorities. Police in Karlsrühe were deeply suspicious of Liszt when he arrived in 1853 wearing a 'democratic' soft wide-brimmed hat of the Kossuth type which had been given him by Wagner. Women who wore the Kossuth shape, which was adapted into 'seaside' hats, were considered dashing and even rather 'fast', but society viewed their lapse of taste with benevolence. In Germany, the broad-brimmed style was known as the 'Letzter Versuch', 'the last attempt', meaning that spinsters wore it in the hope of catching a husband. In sharp contrast, in England the same hat was associated with poets of the social standing of Alfred, Lord Tennyson, Victoria's well-respected laureate.

Hats proclaimed the man – his status, attitudes and beliefs – and the woman – her class, breeding and even matrimonial state. The poke bonnet and the mob cap survived much longer on unmarried (or widowed) heads than on those of married women or girls. What women wore was a question of fashion, but men's clothes were dictated by convention. As the *St James' Gazette* commented in 1890, 'When we are told, "He's a fellow who wears a pot hat and frock coat," we know sufficiently well what sort of fellow he is.' It was understood that no member of polite society would wear a frock coat without the appropriate and sanctioned top

American lady serving tea, 1946.

hat, keeping the pot hat, or bowler, for less formal wear. It was a nineteenth-century rule, as inflexible and immutable, it seemed, as the edict that 'On the afternoon of the Sabbath all respectable men sport a silk topper.' Wall Street and the City were the places where, in honour of the god of money, formality was rigidly applied to the rules of dress, yet after World War I, the inconceivable began to happen even there. Men were seen wearing morning coats with bowlers, a combination that in prewar days would have been the unforgivable sartorial sin.

Not that the bowler, or derby, was an unacceptable hat. It was simply not formal enough for morning coats. After all, was it not the official headwear of upmarket English fishmongers and as clear an indicator of the quality of man and goods as was the straw boater a sure sign of indifferent plaice and somewhat aged cod? There was a 'suitable' hat for every man and each trade and the suitability was weighed on the finest of social scales. To let down one's class by being casual about wearing the dress correct for your situation was as reprehensible as attempting to ape the dress and manners of a class superior to your own. Augustus Sala made the nineteenth-century position clear: 'A "rowdy" hat may be all very well when you are at the seaside . . . or making a tour abroad, but in "society" . . . in paying visits to those whom we hold in some kind of esteem and respect, *the* hat is the stovepipe of the best silk velvet nap.'

It is easy to imagine that the stovepipe, bowler or boater were the only nineteenth-century hats ever worn but, as early as 1822, Lloyd in the Strand was offering forty-eight different styles – and strict rules of etiquette controlled the wearing of each. Even as late as the first decade of the twentieth century, these rules applied. King Edward VII was once asked by the Russian Ambassador if he might attend the races while in mourning. The King replied: 'You may go to Newmarket because a bowler is permissible, but not to the Derby, because a top hat is obligatory.' For Ascot, a grey topper was necessary. Even into the 1930s, when at most race courses bookies wore brown or black bowlers, those at Epsom and Ascot wore full race-going rig, including grey top hats. Today's members of the Jockey Club, when attending race meetings in France, wear black bowlers in deference to the dress codes of French racegoers who, instead of toppers, wear brown or grey bowlers – known as melons – which they obtain from the Parisian hatter Motsch.

Men's hats for social occasions were dictated by custom, but women's were at the mercy of all the swings of fashion – as they still are. The heyday of 'racing' millinery was the period of the Belle Epoque, a period when the Ascot hat – extravagant and stylish – became a separate entity, apart from, though still part of, the rest of the season's millinery. No Henley hat evolved, any more than a Fourth of June hat did. What made Ascot different was its close geographical and social link to the British royal family. It was a proximity that made Ascot pre-eminent as a social occasion. No member of the Royal Ascot Week party could possibly find an excuse not to attend – not that anyone in Edward VII's horse-mad set would have wished to avoid the most stylish of all race meetings.

Edward and Queen Alexandra had created the most fashionable court in Europe, one where clothes and the nuances of their cut and wear were of the greatest importance. The forcing ground for the court's outrageous new fashions was Ascot Week, where the styles were set that would dominate and be copied in more practical form for the rest of the season. For Ascot, crowns grew enormous and brims were extended to balance them. Flowers and feathers – sometimes even whole birds –

French riding fashions of the 1920s.

smothered the lines of all but the most chic hats. For every woman with taste and style enough to consider the line of the hat, there were at least a dozen who decorated to excess. Thus it was that the Ascot hat became known in circles where fashion was truly understood as the extreme hat, verging on vulgarity and worn for show rather than for chic. It has remained so for most of this century. Queen Alexandra, a woman who truly understood fashion and believed in understatement in dress, and King Edward, a stickler for 'form' in fashion, would be horrified at the travesties of the milliner's art which have been paraded since the 1970s for the benefit of the cameras. After his death in 1910, Edward VII was paid the compliment of 'Black Ascot', when every woman wore mourning and trimmed her hat with black feathers, crepe and lace. It was the most elegant Ascot ever and the inspiration for Cecil Beaton's famous black and white Ascot scene in *My Fair Lady*.

But women of the upper classes were not content merely to watch others ride. Although to race was considered eccentric, to hunt was not. As the twentieth century progressed, more and more women took up the sport. The rules for headwear were predictably strict. An early-nineteenth-century manual had laid them down with precision: 'A lady on horseback may wear either a chimney pot, or what the Americans call a stove pipe; a wide-awake, a pork-pie, an Amazon or a "rip-rap".' As hunting became more formal, dress rules insisted that a lady wear copies of men's hats. In 1953 one guide to hunting dress was still insisting that a lady wearing a hunting silk hat should also wear a veil.

When not hunting, a fashionable lady would ride in the Bois du Boulogne, Central Park or Rotten Row, in order to see and be seen. These women were not all 'ladies'. The Achilles Statue in Rotten Row had long been the congregation point for high-class prostitutes, magnificently dressed, in beautifully turned out carriages or mounted on the most high-mettled horses. Known to their clients as 'the pretty horse-breakers', these women were London's fashion leaders. When Skittles, one of Victorian London's most famous prostitutes, appeared in a snappy round-topped riding bowler, all the ladies who condemned her and her trade rushed to follow her lead and a new fashion was created. Rotten Row's smartness was so linked to the quality of the millinery on show there that when informality made hats no longer *de*

French fashion advertisement for 'High Life Tailors', 1913.

rigueur, the old guard resented the change. Sir Walter Gilbey caused a sensation in 1932 with a letter to the *The Times* criticizing 'slovenly' dress: 'I would go so far to give the mounted police orders to ask anyone who appeared in the Row without a hat . . . to retire.'

Undoubtedly, one of the things most resented by Gilbey and his kind was the death of 'hat honour': the doffing of a hat to ladies and gentlemen with whom one was acquainted or to a respected public figure. The rules for 'uncovering' were complex and affected all aspects of life. For example, although a nineteenth-century gentleman would not feel obliged to remove his hat when stepping into his wine merchant's, he would uncover when entering a bank because a banker was not considered to be a tradesperson but a professional man.

In 1889, the Comte de Larmandie spent time observing strollers in the Faubourg Saint Germain in order to note how and when they raised their hats before he sat down to write his guide to 'coup de chapeau'. His rules were, he claimed, based on precedents 'furnished by the most modern and fashionable members of the very best society in Paris'. The man of fashion must remove his hat in saluting 'with a broad sweeping gesture which is at the same time elegant and brusque'. Having held the hat aloft for a while, he must bring it down quickly upon the head, 'like a sword into its scabbard', the whole operation having been performed 'with an impassive countenance'. Such antics must have bored all but the most dedicated followers of social mores and were satirized in 1891 by a pragmatic American who devised a 'novelty' aimed at those who disliked doffing in the cold. The device, as a tongue-in-cheek newspaper report stated, consisted of a hat with a small trapdoor. When an invisible thread was pulled, the trapdoor opened to reveal a tiny figure which bowed and then retired. Readers were assured that this hat was 'much worn in New York just now' by men who could not be bothered to raise their hats.

In their death throes, customs surround themselves with increasingly complex rules. Hat lore was no exception. A manual of 1891 included conventions for every occasion and stated that the hat was no longer lifted by men to one another 'save on occasions when a high official rides by in procession', but it may be 'touched' as a mark of respect. The well-mannered man of 1891 would 'consider the lifting of a hat to him by a male personage as the action of a cad or mendicant', though he was to raise his hat when he was with a lady who bowed to any person, even if 'that person is a total stranger to him'. Hats were always doffed on taking leave of a lady, as a matter of course.

It was not only a question of when but also of how. 'Hat snappers' were the swells who removed their hats and snapped them down suddenly to the waist, holding them upside down. 'Mashers', with their 'big canes, little hats and stony stares', held their heads rigid and forced the hat straight up 'almost at arm's length' before bringing it straight down again. Dignified gentlemen, using the left hand, lifted the hat at an angle and inclined the head forward, 'avoiding all swaggerdom'.

The last decade of the nineteenth century and the first of the twentieth were periods of extravagant display, as fashionable folk in Europe and the United States enjoyed great prosperity and spent huge amounts of money on self-adornment. Men went to the best tailors and hatters and paid what was required to ensure that they had the correct clothing: women spent hours almost daily at their dressmakers and milliners. If a perfectly napped top hat was the pride and joy of the fashionable man, the great status adornment for women's hats were feathers in every shape, size and

colour. Plumassiers in Paris, London and New York demanded huge quantities in order to service the needs of milliners. A single consignment received by a prominent London feather dealer in 1892 illustrates the vast scale: 6,000 bird of paradise feathers, 40,000 humming bird feathers and 360,000 feathers from various birds of the East Indies. It was estimated in the late 1880s that at least five million American birds were killed annually in order to provide hat trimmings. New York trade advertisements were full of references to exotic feathers, many of which had been imported from Paris. Only there, it was felt, could they receive the 'proper' treatment from the plumassiers to the great couture houses.

Wings, aigrettes, breasts, quills and whole birds were dyed, painted and mounted on hats for the fashionable women of the Belle Epoque. The huge slaughter involved touched American consciences first. In 1885 a bill was passed in New Jersey forbidding the killing of any bird 'not generally known as a game bird'. The newly formed national Audubon Society had as a founding principle the prevention of the 'wearing of feathers as ornaments or trimming for dress'. With the turn of the century, the tide had also turned in England. The newly crowned Queen Alexandra let it be known that hats trimmed with feathers of wild birds would not be welcome in her presence. Soon 'acceptable' feathers included only those from domestic birds, such as cockerels, geese or ducks, or specially reared species, such as pheasants or ostriches. The best quality ostrich feathers were taken from living birds and, though one writer pointed out early in the twentieth century that 'with care the bird will pluck well for any number of years, without pain or discomfort', this was obvious propaganda. An anti-feather bulletin from the same period attempted to prick consciences by advising that egret feathers came from the crest of the heron and 'have to be torn from the head of the mother at nesting time and this cruel custom is the cause of death to both mother bird and her young'. But fashion's conscience took

Top left French millinery fashions of the 1920s; *top right La Modiste*, 1905; *above* Turn-of-the-century cartoon satirizing excessive use of feathers in hats.

some time to be moved. Large black velvet hats trimmed with ostrich and called 'Merry Widows' after the heroine of the operetta by Franz Lehar were popular until the first World War, when smaller, sleeker hats became the mode. These led the way to the 1920s supremacy of the cloche which was a runaway fashion success despite the fact that, according to one fashion writer, it 'made the young look forty and the mature, a century'.

John Ruskin referred to women who stuck 'the skins of dead robins' on to their hats as 'disgusting little savages', not, he pointed out, because they were cruel but because they were proud. 'The squire's daughter', he said, 'thinks she looks more like one with a kingfisher or a cockatoo in her cap, which a poor girl cannot get killed for her.' Pride manifested by hats not only troubled artist–philosophers; it had been of consuming concern to the Church for hundreds of years. Womens' hats, decorative and even seductive, presented the Church with a problem. Were they any more suitable to the house of God than the uncovered hair which had, for centuries, been recognized as impermissible in church? Were men committing blasphemy by remaining uncovered? References down the centuries reflect the confusion. In 1581 Peck, in his *Desiderata Curiosa*, noted with disapproval that women wore bonnets in church and men 'sat uncovered'. Bishop Cosin in 1662 expressed concern at those who came to services in Durham Cathedral and sat with their hats on their heads while the lesson was being read. When Archbishop William Laud complained of disorder and bad behaviour in church in the seventeenth century he especially mentioned Puritans who 'march into church and place their hats on the Holy Table'. Even King William gave offence in London by following the Dutch custom of wearing his hat in church during the service.

Confusion over the question of hats in church had been resolved by the beginning of the nineteenth century, although more by custom than by rule. Men removed their hats; women, remaining true to the teachings of St Paul, covered their heads in the presence of God. However, the rules concerning mourning dress became more rigid in the century in which people seemed to be moved as much by the panoply and etiquette of grief as by death itself. The principles regarding mourning headwear were precise and largely concentrated on men's tall hats – worn as a sign of grief even for occasions for which they might not normally be considered necessary. As a writer in the *Hatters' Gazette* in 1892 pointed out, 'For deep mourning . . . the high hat is de rigueur'. The black hatband worn on a mourning hat varied in width according to the status of the deceased. For a widower, a band of 'fine bombazine comes to within one quarter of an inch of the top. For father or mother, one half of an inch from the top. For brother or sister or grown child, three and one half inches up from the brim; and for an aunt, uncle or collateral relation, three and one quarter inches up from the brim.' For all but the last group, the band was expected to be worn for a year. 'Complimentary' mourning for parents-in-law was at the discretion of the mourner but the cynical view was that the bigger the bank account the deeper the mourning, especially for mothers-in-law. For times when tall hats would be inappropriate, mourning bands were to be placed on 'round-topped derbys . . . cheviots, meltons, and any all-black goods that are in good taste.'

For a long time it was customary in England for the sexton to take the clergyman's hat at funeral services, when it was surrounded by huge folds of silk, and place it on a peg behind the pulpit before the sermon began. It remained there as a mark of respect to the dead until the sermon had finished, when it was removed

Victorian mourning hats.

'with dignity and pace'. The custom continued, in rural parishes especially, until well into the 1870s and was retained in Scotland even longer.

Black and death have also been associated in the black cap traditionally worn by judges to pronounce the death sentence. In the sixteenth century, the judge would draw up the flat, square, dark cap that hung at the nape of his neck and, by doing so, conceal his forehead and brow. Eyewitness accounts talk of judges pulling the hood down low to conceal their emotion at pronouncing the penalty of death. Custom was that the judge wore a black cap whenever he gave a judgment in the presence of the monarch, no matter how trivial or severe the sentence. As a young and inexperienced monarch, Queen Victoria was startled when a judge put on his black cap in her presence but, when she queried it afterwards, she was informed that 'even Majesty must respect the majesty of the Law'.

The nineteenth-century obsession with death and its regalia is a proof of the growing insistence on good 'form' that swept through Europe, North America and Great Britain as the rules of social behaviour increasingly became the province of the newly empowered middle classes. Every item of clothing; each style; every manner of wearing an object of dress: all had carefully codified rules. Conclusions were drawn about a man's character as well as his bank balance not only by what he wore but by how he wore it. The manner of wearing the hat was a source of endless speculation. The *New York Post* of 1893, for example, stated that after 'careful, discrete and precise observation', certain generalities about an individual could be inferred from 'the manner in which he wears his chapeau'. The cautious businessman wears his hat exactly on top of his head, giving him a posture 'so stiff as to be awkward'; the careless man wears his hat on the back of his head; and the man who wears his hat on the side of his head is noncommittal. An anonymous writer in the *New York Post* had a different explanation for why hats were worn to the side: 'A well-known titled Englishman', he claimed, 'got on a toot a month ago and, while somewhat exhilarated, appeared upon the Mall with his hat battered in and jammed down on one side of his head and all the boys caught on in a minute.'

English writers came to different conclusions. In a leader, the *Hatters' Gazette* suggested that the hat worn on the back of the head was a sign of brain power as 'it slopes to the back because its owner is without strong animal propensities, which are situated at the back of the head'. The hat placed on the side of the head was the sign of a 'cocky' and self-assertive fellow who 'can handle the billiard-cue, is partial to cards and likes to have a little bit on a horse, about which he thinks he knows more than any man breathing'. If a hat is too large, it betokens the man of a philosophic frame of mind, whereas the small hat is the sign of a 'mincing, affected individual with an inordinate love of dress, and any amount of self-esteem'. Worst of all, by Victorian standards, was the man who threw his hat on at any angle. 'He has', the leader concluded, 'his hands in his pockets and you can see any number of his genus loafing outside public houses and lounging on the street corners.'

When not loafing and lounging, such a man might well be playing a jape that was popular in the United States in the late nineteenth century. This involved slipping a fine sliver of cheese, preferably the strong-smelling limburger, under the sweatband of a friend's hat and waiting for the result as he travelled home from work on a crowded tramcar on a hot summer night. Even without the cheese, the sweatbands of well-used hats tended to smell. The fastidious French, the Paris correspondent of a New York paper reported in the 1890s, had found the answer. Hats of the best quality had a small receptacle hidden beneath the hat leather in which sachets of perfume could be placed so that 'hats may be worn by sudorific customers without giving off that indescribably unpleasant odour which arises from perspiration-soaked linings'. Mindful of his audience, the correspondent concluded that, although the idea might be seen as an 'advance towards effeminacy by our English-speaking nations', it could be distinctly recommended on hygienic grounds. Whether or not an enterprising New York hatter took up his idea is not known. In London, sweatbands created another craze, albeit briefly, at the end of the century when they were made of flexible mica so that 'the wearer may see how he looks when he takes his hat off to a lady'.

In the highly competitive world of hats any novelty for men or 'fancy' for women was considered worthwhile provided it drummed up trade. As advertising was the most successful way of bringing new ideas to the public, manufacturers filled newspapers and periodicals with news of their latest styles. Other means were used only slowly: it was not until 1924 that the first billboard advertising hats appeared, commissioned by the New York firm of Bonar-Phelps.

The most successful notion for stimulating the hat trade was the Easter Parade, an idea dreamed up by New York manufacturers at the end of the Civil War to show off the latest designs in bonnets for women and hats for men. It soon became an institution. Fifth Avenue was blocked off for the day and people of all ages, including children, dressed in their best and paraded their new headwear. Thousands of people were involved and the fillip to the trade was so great that by the 1880s the Easter Parade had become an established tradition in most major U.S. cities. But by the 1930s the idea had become over-commercialized, the hats reduced to mere vehicles for hotel or hot-dog advertising. The Easter Parade began its long decline and by the 1960s it had virtually disappeared.

Commercialization was not the only factor in its decline. It was also the victim of changed attitudes to hats. In 1929 the French dandy André Fouquières laid down that the well-dressed man required fifteen suits, twenty pairs of gloves and at least fifteen hats. By the beginning of World War II such an approach seemed ludicrous. Well-dressed men had stopped following rigid rules. From the 1960s women, too, no longer found hats attractive. Much more exciting were the new ways of creating hairstyles, using one's own hair or wigs. These were not only more modern and therefore more fashionable than hats, but also more comfortable and flexible. In short, they fitted what was seen as 'modern' life in a way that hats no longer could.

At the races, France, 1930s.

AT THE RACES

Royal Ascot is considered the chicest race course in the world; once there, the Royal Enclosure (which packs in 7000 people every day of the week-long meeting) is the chicest place and Thursday is the chicest day. It is Gold Cup Day but is known to everyone as Ladies' Day. On that day, the millinery, which has been excited all week, becomes hysterical and every woman worth her salt wears the hat she is most confident will turn all heads or, even more gratifyingly, all cameras. In such excess a truly elegant hat is rarely, if ever, seen — and, if it were, it would surely be overlooked by novelty-hungry cameramen for whom only the bizarre is noticeable.

Exactly why millinery is such a strong feature of race meetings is a mystery, but unkind theories abound. Some say that women wear extravagant concoctions because they cannot bear to be upstaged by the equine display; others suggest that the fault lies with the men who wish their women to parade their wealth and power like clothes-horses. Whatever the reason, the 'smartness' of a race meeting has, since the 1930s, had little to do with the quality of the racing or the size of the prizes, and everything to do with the elegance of the women who attend.

Above right Prix de Diane, Chantilly, France, 1991

Opposite top Ascot, 1991

Bottom left Chantilly, 1991

Bottom centre David Shilling hat for Ascot, 1980s

Bottom right Chantilly, 1991

Above Bride's Hat Collection, 'Nous Irons Tous au Paradis', silk flowers and tulle, by Marie Mercié, Winter 1988/89

Left Japanese bride in traditional headwear

Opposite Wedding dance, Hungary, 1970

BRIDAL HATS

Bridal headwear has always symbolized the bride's purity and majesty. In Roman times, brides wore yellow veils; in the Middle Ages they garlanded their hair with freshly gathered flowers, but it was not until the 19th century that the bridal wreath and veil of the 'traditional' white wedding evolved. Bridal hats are a 20th-century

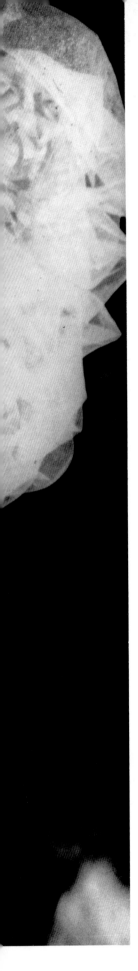

development and vary from a band of flowers (above) to the high-fashion hat (centre) designed by Marie Mercié for her Winter 1988/89 collection. Perhaps most elaborate is the headdress of the Japanese bride (far left), which is often so heavy that she cannot walk unaided. Called a 'tsumo-kakushi', it is designed to hide the horns of jealousy on the wedding day.

LORDS
OF TARTARY

As the horsemen of the Steppes
whirl around at Tartary's equivalent
of Ascot or Saratoga, they are
watched by men wearing what is
possibly the most elegant male
headgear ever devised. But it is
more than that. The richly
embroidered skullcaps and the swirl
of material that holds them in place
are practical as well as beautiful.
They offer protection from the sun
and remain firmly on the head even
when their wearers are out riding.
Here they confer dignity on the
elders watching a boz-kashi (an
entertainment at which riders pursue
at high speed the stuffed carcass of a
goat). This particular event is being
held in honour of the circumcision of
the sons of a local landowner.

Main picture Boz-kashi, display of
horsemanship, Afghanistan

Inset Embroidered skullcaps

TOP HEADS

For most of the 19th century, it was taken for granted that the man of substance showed his superiority by wearing a tall hard hat. The top hat was found on all the 'top heads'. Businessmen, bankers, politicians and all upper-class and aristocratic males wore it for all but the most informal occasions. That they did so is surely proof that men are just as likely to be slaves to fashion as they accuse women of being. By any standards, the top hat is a preposterous headcovering, as uncomfortable as it is inconvenient. It offers perfect proof that people will bear any discomfort in dress provided that they gain prestige and distinction in return.

Although long abandoned as everyday wear, the topper has retained enough social éclat to prevent it from dying out completely. Every year it reappears in all its pomposity and is a perennial favourite for race meetings and weddings. Even now, those who try to break with convention can find themselves frowned upon. Bateman's cartoon 'The Man Who Crept into the Royal Enclosure in a Bowler' (right) was drawn in 1927, but the man's reception would be similar today. The reason is simple: the conventions of dress cannot be exposed to the light of common sense or the whole edifice of fashion and status comes tumbling down.

Left W. Luker, *The Baltic Exchange* (detail), *c.* 1900

Far left below Spaniard in Paris, from E. Texier, *Tableau de Paris*, 1853

Below H. M. Bateman, *The Man Who Crept into the Royal Enclosure in a Bowler*, 1927

FEATHERS

Feathers have adorned prestigious headwear from the ceremonial helmets of the Greeks and Romans to the headdress of American Indians to the hats of the great couturiers. In Henry VIII's time, feathers were modest and vied for attention with the jewels and precious stones that encrusted the fashionable bonnets of courtiers; by the time of Charles II and Henri IV every man of fashion was wearing extravagantly plumed and panached hats of the kind we always associate with English cavaliers and French musketeers. Fashion was not to return to such outrageousness until the fin de siècle, *when the extravagance was found on female rather than male heads. By that time, feathered hats had run so completely out of control that tail feathers – or even a wing – were no longer enough. Fashionable Edwardian ladies frequently demanded the whole bird, stuffed and mounted, as the crowning glory of their hats. The slaughter of birds to answer fashion's demands reached appalling heights. There was a public outcry in the United States and the Audubon Society stopped the trade in wild birds. In 1906 Queen Alexandra announced that she would no longer wear the feathers of wild birds and in 1911, before her official visit to India, Queen Mary disposed of all her plumed millinery.*

But the lure of feathers was not so easily killed and even today milliners love every opportunity to pile them on, thick and high, knowing that the results will be glamorous and exotic. The only difference is that the feathers with which they work are not from endangered species. In fact, most of them are from the humdrum hen, although dyed in every colour a milliner's fancy could ever call for. Their lure, as in Edwardian times, is sexual. They quiver orgasmically with the slightest movement or puff of wind and it has long been assumed that men find the whole thing so arousing that they go weak at the knees.

114

Opposite 'Chapeau de Chantecler', caricature, 1910

Left Feathered crown from Brazil, collected by C. Lévi-Strauss, 1938

Above Hat by Nicholas Oakwell, Spring/Summer 1991

EROTIC HATS

Painters and pornographers have long known that few images are more sexually exciting than the juxtaposition of naked flesh and certain items of clothing. With hats, the frisson comes from teaming an essentially public, formal item of dress with the privacy and intimacy associated with nudity.

Modern filmmakers work with a medium less subtle than paint and their effects are closer to pornography. This still from The Unbearable Lightness of Being *(opposite) has none of the paintings' subtlety. The bowler hat and the décolletage combine to create a strong feeling of sexuality, one that would have been considerably weakened had the actress been wearing a woman's hat, rather than one that is the chief symbol of male sobriety and decorum.*

Right Ernst Ludwig Kirchner, *Semi-Nude Woman with Hat,* 1911

Below Jacques Villon, *Game of Solitaire,* 1903

Opposite Still from *The Unbearable Lightness of Being,* 1987

HERMES

It seems totally fitting that Hermès, makers of the world's most prestigious headscarves, should create a scarf decorated with classic hat shapes, since their product has, for many women, taken the place of the hat.

The firm was founded in 1857 by Thierry Hermès, a saddler, who opened a shop in Paris to provide harnesses and sporting accessories for the carriage trade. The quality of workmanship was so high that Hermès was soon providing equipage for most of the crowned heads and aristocrats of Europe. Surprisingly, though the firm produced riding crops, gloves and boots, it never made riding hats. But its famous equestrian scarves have made the name Hermès synonymous with quality for the past one hundred years. Extravagantly large, and beautifully printed on the finest silk, a Hermès scarf is a collector's item, appreciated by all women who love luxury at its purest.

'Chapeau', headscarf by Hermès

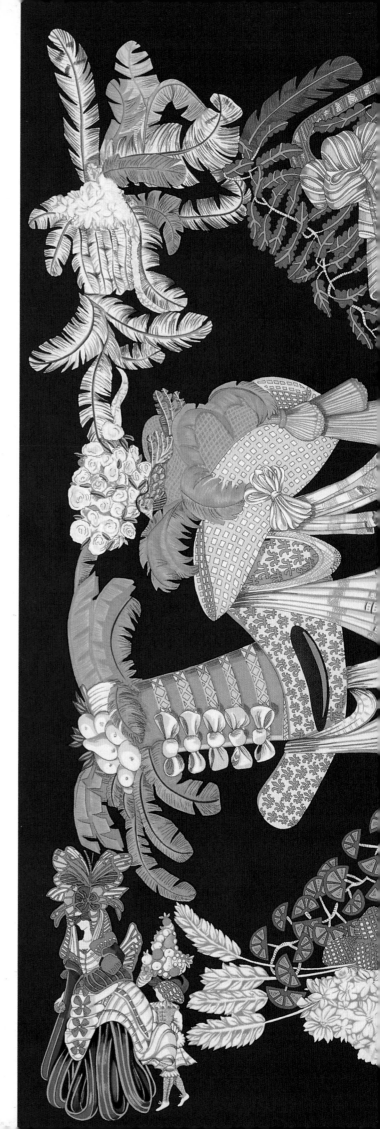

*F*or fashionable society, hats serve little purpose except to flatter the wearers and make their social status manifest. For workers, headcoverings are more serious. They are there for protection rather than projection. Appearance is secondary to safety. Essentially practical and pragmatic, working hats have evolved not in answer to fashion's dictates but in response to individual climatic and working conditions.

But though it may originally have been conceived as a purely practical solution to a specific problem, no item of dress remains that simple for long. In Western cultures, working hats have frequently developed their own form of status, and have been used to show the rank and profession of the wearer. They have often been copies of fashionable headwear, such as the top hat, or slightly old-fashioned versions of hats once considered the prerogative of the gentleman, as in the case of the servant's cocked hat worn long after it had been abandoned by the master.

Between the gentlemen and the workers – the ditch diggers, coal heavers, sowers and reapers – hovered the domestic servants. Until the twentieth century, vast numbers of people were employed as servants and their dress was carefully calculated to be part of a nicely balanced triangle reflecting the status of the employer, the deference of the employee and the practical demands of work. In short, the employer wished to dress his servants so that he could feel proud without encouraging pride in *them*: an uppity servant was a cross that many an eighteenth-century employer found hard to bear. Earlier, personal servants had not posed such a problem as they were usually drawn from the 'gentleman' class, though they were always subject to constricting rules of dress. For example, not even high ranking servants were permitted to remain hatted indoors in the presence of their master and servants who wore hats that were too fancy were seen as a reflection of their masters' slackness. Even the Pilgrim Fathers were not entirely egalitarian in this matter. Eighteenth-century edicts against allowing servants to dress above their station are almost as frequently found in the New World as in the Old.

Nevertheless, a certain controlled extravagance was permitted. A senior servant's hat, after all, like the rest of his livery, was meant to reflect the wealth and power of his master, and money spent to produce grandeur was considered to be well-spent. Hats laced with gold and decorated with gilt buttons were as commonplace in the

Fur hats, Moscow, 1991.

grandest houses of Philadelphia as in those of London or Berlin and even the servants of the 'middling sort' were dressed to impress as much as their masters' incomes would allow.

By the first years of the eighteenth century, cockaded hats had become the badge of authority for the senior servant – they still survive today in the grand hotel commissionaire's cockaded high hat. W. D. Vincent explained the genesis of the cockade in his *British Livery Garments*, published in the 1890s. Cockades worn by army and navy officers were also sported by their servants in order to show that, although not in uniform, they also were soldiers and sailors. Later, the private servants of officers in the two services adopted them. They spread into civilian life and became a commonplace of the senior servant's hall on both sides of the Atlantic. Cockades were always worn on the left side of the hat and were rosette-shaped. For weddings in England servant's cockades were white; otherwise they were normally black or dark blue.

The power associations of the tall silk livery hat, 'heavier than the ordinary style and,' according to Vincent, 'made more with the view of exposure to bad weather than the ordinary kind', meant that it became the hat of authority when worn by servants and workers just as it was when worn by gentlemen. Throughout the nineteenth century it was permitted for certain senior public servants whose job brought them into contact with the people and whose role was to impose order and control. The dress associated with the railways is an example. The importance and power of this novel form of transport, which so frightened Queen Victoria that she forbade the royal train to travel faster than 40 miles per hour and insisted on making frequent eating stops, was echoed in the demeanour and dress of those responsible for its efficient running. Guards and stationmasters came directly into contact with the public and were dressed not only to impress, but also to inspire confidence in what was initially considered to be a potentially dangerous method of travel. The natural headwear for such important officials was the top hat but, this being too tall to be worn inside the train, guards wore caps with steeply sloping peaks. Known as cheese cutters, they were based on the service dress cap and this in itself lent them authority. Although less imposing than top hats, they did not lack grandeur. They were frequently laced with gold and their brims were usually decorated with silver or gold piping. When, in the 1860s, patent leather brims became standard, they invariably had some kind of metallic, quasi-military decoration to them.

Stationmasters preferred dignity to gaudiness and at mainline stations they saw trains off on time in frock coats or adaptations of military dress uniform. In England the stationmaster wore the top hat of the gentleman to reflect the importance of his office. It was the headwear of authority, and even as late as the 1930s, when top hats had all but disappeared from the streets, they were still worn by stationmasters of mainline London stations if someone of political or social importance were travelling. In the great railway stations of Europe, such as Munich and Milan, a stationmaster's authority was proclaimed in a more military style. The earliest railway headwear was based on the shako, but it was soon modified (as military headwear was) to bring in the kepi, braided and decorated according to the rank of the official. It was, however, frequently higher than the military version so that an official would stand out from the crowd.

Passengers, like guards, found it difficult to move through carriages in a top hat. To solve the problem, two pieces of cord were stretched across first-class carriages

Below Livery hat with gold band and cockade, 1881; *bottom* From a Grandville cartoon showing master and page as lion and cub, 1840s.

above the heads of the seated passengers. The toppers were slipped under the cords and hung upside down, in a row. They must have looked rather like resting bats as trains trundled across country in the dusk. The railway and the top hat took some time to come to terms with each other: in the early days trains frequently had to be stopped so that male passengers could retrieve their lost hats from the side of the line. The few women intrepid enough to venture on to a train wore their bonnet strings extra tight in case the wind might blow away the protection of their modesty. Newspaper reports of the official opening of new lines often felt it sufficiently newsworthy when describing inaugural runs to mention the fact that 'nobody's hat blew off'.

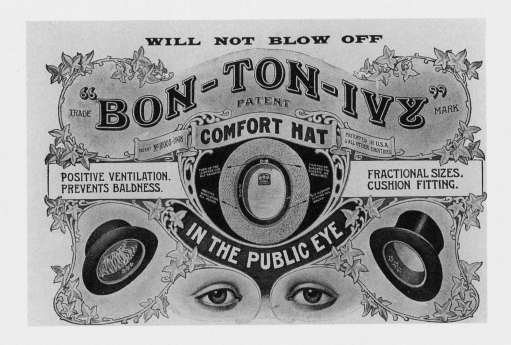

Advertisement from the *Hatter's Gazette*, 1910.

Stationmasters were not alone in requiring the status of a tall hat. The chef's hat is little more than a topper done in white and it did not evolve into its modern form until the top hat had become *the* shape of nineteenth-century power. Previously, chefs had worn hats that were practical rather than showy. Head cooks in fashionable restaurants and gentlemen's clubs from Boston to Bristol were well aware of their importance and power in a century when public eating and the quality of food came to the fore. Ease of foreign travel made the rich more discerning and increasingly snobbish. In the United States and England such snobbery manifested itself in a cultural belief that all good things came from France. It was assumed that French chefs, like French dressmakers, were of superior skills. Further, they brought cachet to their employer. Even the traditional English aristocracy and Establishment were not immune: Antoine Carème worked for Lord Stewart and Alexis Soyer was the chef at the Reform Club in London. It was while Lord Stewart was British Ambassador in Vienna in 1820–21 that Carème, who had accompanied him there, changed the ordinary white cap worn by chefs into something rather more like the modern chef's hat. For most of history no rules of hygiene existed which compelled cooks to cover their heads in the kitchen and, in fact, they rarely wore any form of headwear at all. In the early nineteenth century, bakers had adopted a flat white tam-o'-shanter, but this was for practical rather than hygienic

The baker's hat, from which the chef's hat evolved. Advertisement for Birds' Custard Powder, 1895.

reasons – it enabled trays of pastries and bread to be safely carried on the head, while protecting the skull from their heat.

Carême's adaptation of the baker's flat hat was cosmetic rather than practical. He wished to create a hat more in keeping with his importance than the floppy tam-o'-shanter shape generally worn by cooks and, having noticed a girl in Vienna wearing a stiff white cap, he copied the idea by stiffening a traditional nightcap with a circlet of cardboard. Lord Stewart was impressed and complimented his chef. The stiffened cap swept through the grander kitchens of Europe and North America and a fashion statement – for the effects were purely aesthetic – had been made. Further, it was the first step in the irresistible rise of the chef's covering in its attempt to catch up with the topper. Many experiments in cutting, starching and pleating later, the twentieth-century chef's high white starched cap appeared. French tradition states that it should have one hundred pleats to represent the number of different ways in which a great chef can prepare eggs.

If the chef wore the white hat, the master chef frequently did no such thing. As if to emphasize the fact that he was far too grand to stand sweating over a stove, Alexis Soyer supervised the underchefs at the Reform Club wearing a black velvet beret with a tassel. He was soon copied by many of the master chefs of top hotels and restaurants in London and Paris.

The stiffened high hat was clearly better able to protect the head than a soft-topped cap. Perhaps that is why British policemen adopted it. The first uniformed policemen in England were appointed in 1750 by the novelist Henry Fielding, when he was Chief Magistrate at Bow Street in London. The force was disbanded through lack of funds, and it was not until 1805 that the idea of a paid permanent police force was revived by Sir John Ford, who instituted the Bow Street Mounted Horse Patrol, a night patrol, known as 'Robin Redbreasts' because of their scarlet waistcoats. Their hats were high, to give them an imposing appearance, and made of leather, to protect their heads. In 1822 Sir Robert Peel instituted a day foot patrol: the Bow Street Runners, the first uniformed police force in the world.

Although the Bow Street uniform was not consciously based on military wear, its links with naval uniform struck observers at the time, one of whom commented that the hat 'was probably just homely enough to save the day'. A six-inch high, wide-brimmed stovepipe, it had a black leather top and was reinforced with cane. In extremis – though these facts were not mentioned in manuals – it could be used as a weapon, a shield for the face and a stepping stone across water or when climbing a wall. Nevertheless, it was not a sensible hat for the job: the sun cracked the leather top; the rain made the beaver crown and brim look shabby and, worst of all, it needed a hand to hold it on when a constable was in pursuit of a criminal. In 1863 the Metropolitan police of London were issued with helmets. Made of cork and covered with serge, they were the precursors of the modern British policeman's helmet. They were an amalgam of civilian and military design, being based on Russian and Prussian army helmets and the newly popular bowler. The earliest models were 'combed', with a raised spine for extra strength running from the top to the back, and a curled brim. Those made by Knox of London were so famous in the 1880s that they were exported worldwide. The firm made all the helmets for the New York City Police Force for several years.

Because police forces in the nineteenth century were allowed a considerable degree of autonomy with regard to uniforms – often answering to local rather than national authorities – they indulged in many variations. These were frequently based on nothing more official than the idiosyncrasies of individual chief constables and their desire for personal and force grandeur. Military-style embellishments proliferated: brass chin straps, large metallic badges and impressive finials, spikes and rosettes were not confined to the chief constable's ceremonial headwear. They frequently appeared on the helmet of the policeman on the beat. However, towards the end of the century, the British model was no longer the main pattern for other police forces. Whereas the British bobby continued to wear the high-domed military-style helmet, other police forces had begun the transition to the more practical modern peaked cap, now universal except in the United Kingdom and some Commonwealth countries. The years of transition at the turn of the century saw European policemen wearing high, straightsided peaked helmets based more on the French kepi than on the British model.

Not so American police of the kind who menaced Chaplin, or the Keystone Cops who were endlessly having their helmets knocked off by lawless members of society. They continued to wear helmets almost indistinguishable from their British prototype until well into the 1920s. Initially, the service dress cap style was reserved for wear by chief constables and senior officers; the policeman on the beat always wore a helmet. The change from helmet to cap for all was initiated in America when motorized police were first used. Police cars made high helmets impractical and they became even less useful when motor bike patrols were introduced in the twenties. They were eventually abandoned in favour of the more practical cap which was soon taken up by other forces in place of the kepi. Even before the beginning of the 1930s, the British were the only police force still wearing the high helmet. Today, their helmets – quaint, impractical and strangely unmenacing – have made them a tourist attraction. Most modern police forces have opted for the cap, although some, like the Spanish Civil Guard and the French police, have chosen to retain the stiffened kepi for everyday wear. The Italian Caribinieri, founded in 1814, after Piedmont became free of French rule, still wear the Napoleonic bicorne for ceremonial occasions.

Early fire officer's hats shared many characteristics with those of the police and a style emerged in London in the seventeenth century that became the model for firefighters in different countries. Of leather, with raised ribs for extra strength and a protective flap for the back of the neck, it was practical, but heavy. By 1800, the lighter beaver hat became popular and, by 1830, it had taken on the characteristics of the stovepipe. When the London Metropolitan Fire Brigade was formed in 1866, the Chief Fire Officer, Eyre Massey Shaw, designed a brass helmet for the men, based on the helmet of the French Sapeurs-Pompiers, with a white metal version for officers. The new helmet was not immediately adopted universally and, throughout the century, many forces continued to use leather helmets.

In the United States, credit for inventing the first leather fire cap goes to Jacobus Turch, who was appointed caretaker of the first New York fire engine in the 1740s. Most of the early fire hats were made by saddlers such as Mathew du Bois, who expanded his business by opening a factory in New York in 1824 specifically to make hats for the firefighting companies that had sprung up across the country. However, the best known supplier of firefighter's hats in the nineteenth century was Henry T. Gatacap, who set himself up as a specialist manufacturer in 1836 and made hats for most U.S. fire brigades for the next thirty years. He was the man who introduced the rigidly stitched seams, or combs, the number of which dictated the cost (and the

Top Military helmet, *c.* 1905; *above* Standard British policeman's helmet.

durability) of the hat. Gatacap made 'one-offs' for presentation to fire chiefs and these were often remarkably fancy: when the voluntary firemen of Sacramento, California, decided to present a ceremonial helmet to their fire chief, Gatacap created a version with an elaborate gold and silver badge encrusted with precious stones, for which he charged $1,350. Few helmets were so embellished and, for everyday firemen, the only additional decoration was a wreath of oak leaves around the crown of the helmet, signifying that the wearer had saved a life. But such extravagances were rare. Practicality took precedence over fantasy in a field where the correct uniform could make the difference between life and death. It is for this reason that there is so little variation in the helmets of the world's firefighters.

Although workers wish to appear imposing if at all possible, fitness of purpose comes first. That is why porters in Covent Garden or Les Halles attached a 'knot' to their hats. A supporting pad, it helped balance and spread the weight of the boxes of fruit and vegetables that were frequently carried on the head. Meat and fish porters also carried their goods on their heads. Their hats were made of leather both for extra strength and to protect the hair from dripping liquids. The 'billycock' worn by fish porters in London's Billingsgate was considered the most macho hat of the English hat business. Most were bought from Edward Spink, of Love Lane, in London's East End, and they were bought for life. Weighing about five pounds and constructed for durability, they did, literally, last for a working life, even though they were never washed or cleaned as it was feared that this would bring bad luck.

Billingsgate, like most fish markets, probably took some of its superstitions from those of sailors and fishermen. Certainly, the practice of not washing a hat would be familiar to sailors, who were used to tarring their hats against the effects of salt, sea, wind and rain – an activity that in England earned them the title of 'Jack Tars'. Admiral Sir Cyprian Bridge recalled in his memoirs watching sailors in the 1850s plaiting their own hats from sennit. Each sailor made two, one of white untreated straw, and the other, covered in calico, thickly coated with tar or black paint for protection against salt and sun. The shape of the flat-brimmed round sailor hat, known in the United States as a pie cap, had become standard in Europe by the end of the nineteenth century and, with minor variations, continues so to this day. American naval authorities took a more practical approach during World War I and introduced for ordinary wear the circular washable white cap known worldwide for its associations with Popeye.

On land, the need for protection against the elements was also a major consideration for farmworkers, shepherds, wood-cutters and all who worked in the open. Few rural workers went about their business bareheaded. Cheap, serviceable headwear was required by people who, traditionally, were more poorly paid than most workers. The description of Piers Plowman's hood as 'full of holes' could apply to the dress of most European farm labourers from the Middle Ages until well into the eighteenth century. Their hats were often home-made, using any material that was plentiful and cheap. Knitted caps were common but straw and felt hats were also used as early as the fifteenth century. In colder climates – Russia, Central Europe and North America – primitive fur hats were widespread. The version most familiar to us is the nineteenth-century North-American Davy Crockett hat, originally made from raccoon fur. At the opposite climatic extreme, the Breton beret, taken up in the nineteenth century by Bohemians, artists and writers because of its practicality and lack of status connotations, was originally used by farmers in Northern France to protect their heads from the sun. Nineteenth-century agricultural workers in North America frequently tied a bandanna around their large-brimmed hats so that they could use it to wipe the sweat from their faces. In Australia, the men of the outback tied corks to the brims of their hats in order to keep off flies. By the eighteenth century, the bullycock hat, later known as the billycock, had become common wear for farmers in England. It was superseded by the all-powerful stovepipe in the early nineteenth century but was soon reinstated as the 'Billy' or Derby, popular in the upper levels of agricultural workers – the overseers, farm managers, flour millers and sawmill proprietors – of Europe and America until well into the twentieth century.

Women servants, both in the fields and indoors, hid their hair in a cap or hat. This was as much a mark of their respectability and modesty as a protection against dust or dirt. In this they were following the lead of their social superiors, since all women were expected to cover their hair at all times. The mob cap was universal in the eighteenth century and lasted in country districts and as part of the dress of elderly women until well into the nineteenth century. An indoor cap of cambric or muslin with a frilled border, it was originally tied under the chin by 'kissing strings' although, by the middle of the eighteenth century, these had disappeared and the cap fitted the head loosely, kept in place by a ribbon band. The mob cap was often worn with a flat straw hat in summer.

During the nineteenth century the mob cap changed, developing a brim and side panels (like a poke bonnet but without the stiffening) which protected the back of the neck from the sun. It was to become the archetypal milkmaid's bonnet, familiar from paintings and still in existence well into the twentieth century as the child's sunbonnet. Although the milkmaid worked in this bonnet, she adopted a more impressive style when she set off to sell her milk. Normally, she wore the flat chip straw bergere of the countrywoman on top of her cap but, in London at least, some milk sellers wore the tall hat that has since become associated with Welsh national dress. In fact, throughout the eighteenth century, men and women in Wales wore round-crowned felt hats and it was not until the 1820s that a taller hat began to be worn. The hat now considered part of the national costume was largely the mid-nineteenth-century invention of Augusta Hall, later Lady Llanover, as part of her dual campaign to promote a national costume and encourage the tourist trade. Although it caught on for a time, it was never everyday wear, being largely kept for 'special' occasions such as Sundays and market days.

The day of the artificially created Welsh hat for women was brief; that of the paper hat, a truly practical improvisation in answer to a real problem for many working men, was not. The paper hat was first adopted in the nineteenth century by carpenters who needed a cool, lightweight, cheap headcovering to keep shavings and fine wood-dust out of their hair. Small and square, it fitted the head rather like a pillbox and was

An English housekeeper, 1886.

easily made each morning from the previous day's newspaper or a piece of old brown paper. Paper hats were by no means confined to woodworkers. Many indoor trades adopted them, especially when the cost of paper came down and newspapers became larger and more plentiful. The paper cap was essentially a manual worker's hat found on the heads of plasterers, plumbers and printers and still worn today by *muratori* – Italian bricklayers and builders. But it was also worn in certain shops, though only by the most lowly employees. Charles Dickens, in *David Copperfield*, pinpoints its lack of status in his description of the head boy in a wine merchant's shop: 'His name was Mick Walker, and he wore a ragged apron and a paper cap.'

For centuries, the hard hat of the jockey and riding man was the nearest sport came to protective clothing but, in this century, when sporting activities have not only become more competitive but also much faster, the need for protection has been felt even in games as traditionally non-aggressive as cricket. Wicket keepers were always considered most at risk and, after the controversial 'Bodyline' tour of Australia in 1933, Patsy Hendren invented the first protective headgear for the game: a leather helmet which turned out to be too uncomfortable to wear. However, the idea was revived in 1976 by Mike Brearley and Tony Grieg who, aware that a modern cricket ball can come off the pitch at speeds of up to 100 m.p.h., wore helmets under their caps. These, provided by a firm specializing in surgical appliances, were made of polyethylene, cast from a wax mould of the player's head.

Comfort and protection were also required in the helmets of American football players. Early models were copied from leather flying helmets, but these were very heavy and were abandoned in the late 1930s in favour of a lighter plastic helmet. Early plastic models had a tendency to split, so later examples used reinforced plastic for the shell and lined it with shock-absorbing foam. Many modern helmets have shock-absorbing inflatable bladders inside the shell. Jockey's helmets, too, have become more effective; they are now made from glass fibre with the surface sanded and coated with white paint so that their caps will not slip off during a race.

The pace and danger of modern life, on or off pitch, playing field or racecourse, would surely terrify people from previous centuries where the rhythm of society was dictated by the horse. Until well into the twentieth century, horses provided transport and haulage in city and country alike and it is not surprising that, in the main, they were carefully looked after. And even horses had their hats. In the late nineteenth century it was considered right for an ambitious coachman to look around and make a careful choice of headgear for his horse, in order to get something to suit it. The range was surprisingly wide, from bell-shaped linen hats with earpieces of the same material to straw sugarloaf hats with broad brims, which protected the neck and brow. These were often trimmed with coloured ribbon, with a cockade at one side. Hats for horses caught on not only in animal-loving Britain and hot countries such as Spain and Italy; they were especially popular in Germany. In 1900 the Berlin Omnibus Company made them standard summer wear for their horses.

But of course it was left to the English to carry the idea to its extreme. In the 1920s it became a fad to provide dogs with protective headwear. The *Hatters' Gazette* commended the choice available in 1924 and suggested that 'white, brown, dark blue or speckled, shepherd's plaid' or whatever, should be chosen 'according to the colour and physiognomy of the dog'. But it added, wisely enough, 'One can hardly expect a great future for this adornment.'

Rural worker, Andalusia, 1950s.

HEADSCARVES

The headscarf is the simplest and most flexible female headcovering. Almost entirely enveloping the hair, it imparts a sense of decency and modesty. Yet it is frequently a highly decorative form of dress. Traditional cotton kerchiefs favoured by European peasant women are printed with lively patterns and complex designs in bold, powerful colours. Worn on feast days and holidays, they are still an important part of ethnic dress.

The most famous scarves of the 20th century are probably those worn by Queen Elizabeth. Although these have been criticized as dowdy and dull, the Queen continues to wear them because, like any countrywoman, she knows that headscarves are practical and perfectly adaptable to outdoor life.

Headscarves do not have to be unsophisticated. In the 1960s the Italian designer Emilio Pucci manufactured silk scarves based on the strong colours and bold patterns of medieval banners which were an instant success with the international fashion world. His lead has been followed with great success by the French firm Hermès, the Italian company Gucci and, most recently, by the couturier Gianni Versace.

This page Carl Wilhelmson, *Fisherwoman on the Way to Church* (detail), 1899

Opposite left Romania, 1976

Opposite right top Ruskin Spear, *The Headscarf*, c. 1978

Opposite right below Mink headscarf by Balenciaga, Winter 1965

Background Women in a Transylvanian village, Romania

THE HOOD

For such an essentially practical form of headwear the hood
can be remarkably mysterious and pure. In the hands of
couturiers of the calibre of Cristobal Balenciaga (below)
and Issey Miyake (opposite), it has the same sculptural
beauty as the nun's coif or an elaborate piece of origami. The
early hood with the liripipe shares the same quality, as the
14th-century example excavated in Greenland reveals
(below right). It could be shown by any modern couturier
and would be applauded for its elegance and simplicity. The
even earlier example from Iran (right) could also be worn by
a modern woman and receive nothing other than praise for its
stylishness. Both go to prove that good design does not date
and that certain shapes evolve so perfectly that they serve for
all time.

Above right Scythian gold plaque, 5th century BC

Right 14th-century liripipe hood excavated at the
Norse cemetery of Herjolfsnoes, Greenland

Below Balenciaga, Winter 1967

Opposite Issey Miyake, Tokyo collection, Spring/
Summer 1989

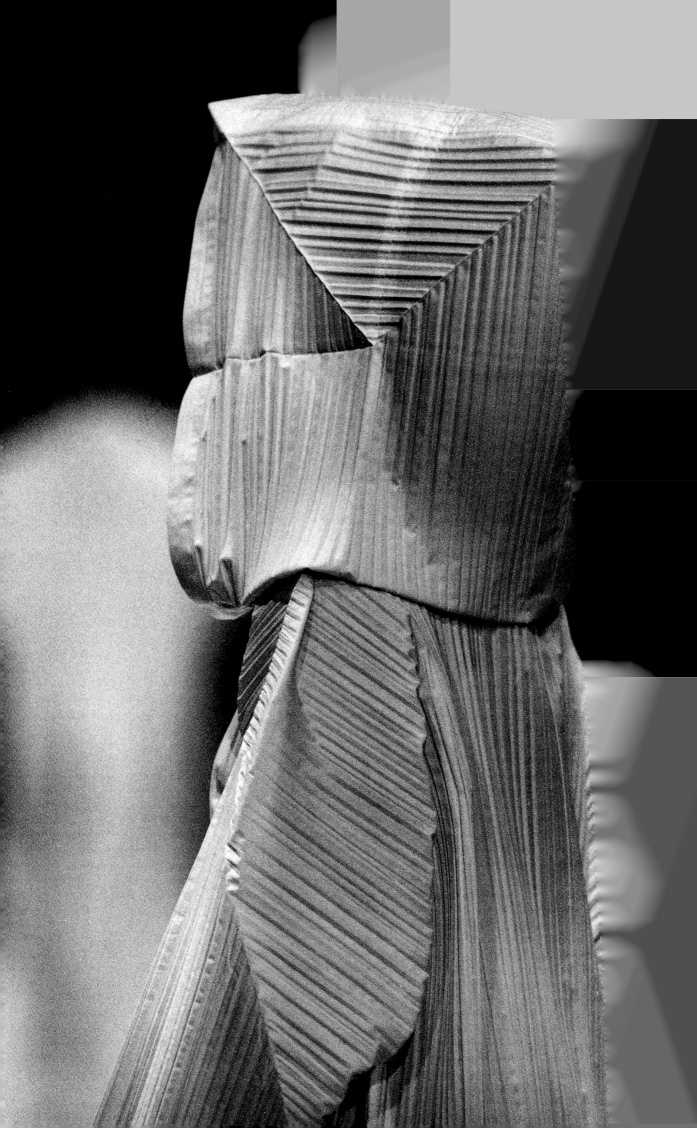

THE VEIL

The veil is the only headcovering that is exclusive to one sex. Its wear has always been confined to women. It has been worn from the earliest times and is still a vital item of clothing for all women whose religion demands that their hair and frequently their complete head be kept covered in public. It betokens modesty but can also suggest the allure of the hidden and unattainable. The woman in Kabul wearing the traditional chadri (opposite) is as far removed from fashion and its variants as the lady from the 18th-century Gallery of Fashion (left) is completely a part of the world of la mode. Whereas the Afghanistani woman's veil protects her from male gazes, the ostrich feather and veil of the woman in the fashion plate are clearly designed to attract the attention of all who pass by. John Galliano's 1988 version (left) has a little of both approaches. Although eye-catching, his swirl of tulle has an innocent freshness that is the antithesis of blatant display.

Above left Veil with ostrich feather, *Gallery of Fashion*, 1794

Left John Galliano, Spring/Summer 1988

Opposite Afganistani woman in Kabul, wearing the traditional *chadri*

THE COCKED HAT

The tricorne, or three-cornered hat, evolved as the practical solution to a problem rather than as a preconceived fashion. Eighteenth-century soldiers found wide-brimmed protective hats inconvenient in that the brims tended to flop over the eyes. To stop this happening they cocked them back off the brow. A style was thus created which was taken up by fashionable men everywhere and was frequently adopted by

Top Philip Mercier, *Sir Edward Hales*, 1744

Centre 'Folding the tricorne', *The Hatmaker's Shop*, 1765

Right C. W. E. Dietrich (1712–74), *Lady with Straw Hat*

Above J.-L. David, *Bonaparte Crossing the St Bernard Pass*, c. 1800

Opposite Jean-Paul Gaultier, Spring/Summer 1992

women. The tricorne was one of the most popular hats in the history of men's fashion and it fell from grace not because a new style took its place but because wigs grew so large that hats became redundant, except for show.

The hat that replaced the tricorne was the chapeau bras. Designed more to be carried than to be worn, the chapeau bras was folded flat and tucked under the arm. It was a style favoured by Napoleon, who wore a theatrically braided and cockaded example for his romanticized portrait by J.-L. David. It is because of its romantic and theatrical associations that the bicorne is regularly revised by avant-garde couturiers who are not only attracted to its stylish shape but also find it to be a perfect vehicle for playing games with fashion historicism.

SEASIDE HATS

The straw hat has always symbolized freedom from formality and the joys of the outdoor life – especially those of the seaside. As early as the 18th century, when the sea was just beginning to be associated with pleasure, the straw hat became the fashionable way to protect the skin from the sun's injurious rays. Small and modestly proportioned, the traditional seaside straw was designed in the knowledge that strong winds were as much a feature of seaside life as the sun was.

It is only in the 20th century that the extravagantly trimmed sunshade straw hat has become fashionable. Its popularity reflects the fact that for many modern holiday-makers the 'seaside' now includes tropical beaches. In such a climate, protection against the sun is crucial and the likelihood of gale-force winds can be discounted. Jacques Heim's raffia hat from the 1940s (right) looks as if it has been lifted entire from the roof of a tropical beach hut and Sybilla's late 1980s version (opposite) mimics the patterns left on the sand by retreating waves. Both hats have the glamour that large-scale brims always give but, more importantly, they are lighthearted and fun – which is what the seaside, no matter how exotic, is still all about.

Far left 'Bathing place', *Gallery of Fashion*, 1796

Left Paddling, England, 1890s

Below Hat by Sybilla, late 1980s

Below left Hat by Jacques Heim, 1940s

Top Poster for Buffalo Bill's
Wild West, 1898

Right James Dean

Opposite Hat by Patricia
Underwood, 1991

THE HAT THAT CROWNED THE WEST

The stetson, 'the hat that crowned the West', was invented by U.S. hatmaker John B. Stetson in the 1860s. The style was to take the cowboy hat market by storm and turn Stetson into a multi-millionaire.

Buffalo Bill's Roadshow made the stetson hat a vital prop for showbusiness cowboys. Screen stars such as Tom Mix, Gene Autry and Roy Rogers later popularized it for outdoor wear for the American man and over the years it has been adopted by many U.S. politicians, including Dwight D. Eisenhower, Lyndon B. Johnson and Ronald Reagan.

The last time the cowboy hat was seen on the screen as a convincing symbol of masculine sexuality was when it was worn by James Dean in George Stevens's film of Edna Ferber's novel Giant in 1957. The particular cock of his brim was as provocative as any given by an 18th-century soldier to his tricorne.

The cowboy hat has often been borrowed by designers and milliners for wear by women. Vivienne Westwood adapted it for her Buffalo collection in the mid-1980s and Patricia Underwood recaptured its elegantly simple shape in her collection for 1991.

THE
CAP OF SERVICE

It is often forgotten that military uniform has been the source of a variety of male fashions, especially in headwear. The 18th-century tricorne worn by every gentlemen for almost one hundred years was originally a military style. The shako and kepi both provided inspiration for working uniforms in the 19th and early 20th century – the kepi is clearly the origin of the Victorian guard's cap (opposite). But it is the army officer's service cap (seen left *in its 1918 version) which has been in recent times the most copied item of military dress. It is worn by chauffeurs, doormen, janitors and security guards, all of whom benefit from its associations with authority and duty.*

Opposite Guard at London station, 1885

Top Service cap by Bates, London, 1918

Above Knightsbridge, London, 1953

*T*he idea that Paris is the source of all fashion innovation and style developed as long ago as the eighteenth century, when Marie Antoinette sold her soul, and eventually the crown of her husband's realm, to her milliner, Rose Bertin. Bertin is one of the handful of dressmakers working before the rise of the couturier at the end of the nineteenth century to have come down to us by name. Most of these women were modest, hard-working and subservient. They realized that they must fear the frown of the great, hold no opinions and do as they were told. Socially, they hovered in the nether regions of the middle classes, half trusted servant, half lowly artisan. Their names and reputations died with them.

Rose Bertin may well have begun her career in this twilight zone of genteel respectability but she did not remain there. More ambitious and possibly more creative than the rest of her kind, she was clearly an exceptional businesswoman with an intuitive understanding of the 'ton' of the times, which in fact she largely created. Born in Abbeville in 1747, she was in Paris working for a milliner by the time she was sixteen. Her skill in designing toilettes showed itself early; her flair for personal publicity and self-aggrandisement only became apparent later. The style of her creations pleased the fashion leaders of the time and, encouraged by their enthusiasm, Rose Bertin set herself up as a *marchande de modes* in the rue du Faubourg Saint-Honoré in 1770. *Marchands de modes* occupied the area between shopkeeper and dressmaker. They sold ribbons, lace and trimmings for toilettes, but also frequently dressed a woman from their own stock. It was at this that Bertin excelled. Her shop soon became famous for its witty suggestions as to how to use the latest ribbons, how to wear the newest lace and how to decorate the hat of the moment.

In the stultifyingly boring world of fashionable life at Versailles, trapped in a sterile round of social events centred on a pompous and humourless king, anything amusing, outrageous or merely different enough to engage jaded imaginations for even a day caught on like wildfire. Everyone talked, everyone came to look, many stayed to praise, most actually bought. Rose Bertin was perhaps the first originator of the modern concept of 'must haves'. She made it her business to be the first with new ideas and to present them with such audacity that they became 'must sees' for the whole of Paris and 'must buys' for the majority of the fashionable clique. She was

The height of fashion, Paris, 1909.

Marie Antoinette (*above*) and
her milliner, Rose Bertin
(*right*).

a great opportunist who kept her ear to the ground, always knew the latest gossip
and usually found a way to capitalize on it. For example, when Louis XVI was
inoculated in 1774, the whole of Paris was full of speculation. Rose Bertin created a
'pouf à l'inoculation' headdress, displaying a wit that delighted her patrons. When
The Marriage of Figaro was the success of Paris, she made a 'toque à la Suzanne' to
celebrate Baumarchais' heroine.

Bored, pampered, desperately in need of diversion, the royal ladies, their
aristocratic attendants, the beaux of the moment and all the ragtag and bobtail who
cling to the skirts of the fashionable world found that a visit to Rose Bertin could be
the highlight of the day. But, important as their attentions were, it was on the smile
of the Queen that Rose Bertin waited. It was bestowed with increasing regularity.
The two women became more and more intimate, differences in rank and fortune
forgotten in their obsession with fashion and their mutual, all-consuming vanity.
The Queen adored clothes; Bertin equally adored her position of power. More
closely involved with Marie Antoinette than were many of France's top nobility, she
was in the happy position of being solicited for snippets of royal gossip, pointers as
to what direction royal taste was taking and help in suggesting how court ladies
might ingratiate themselves into the inner circle that danced attendance on the
Queen. As Rose Bertin became rich, she became arrogant, charging the highest
prices in Paris and frequently insulting her customers. Her behaviour preshadowed
the excessive, even comic, grandeur that was to arrive one hundred years later with
the posturings and pomposities of the couturiers Worth and Poiret.

Bertin's strength was based on wealth as well as on talent. She became a rich
woman because Marie Antoinette was the archetypal fashion victim, a compulsive
buyer who could not say no, even when she must have known that her enormous
bills had become unacceptable. Her role and its function fed – and almost justified –
her obsession. Aileen Ribeiro in her illuminating study, *Dress in Eighteenth-Century
Europe*, points out how many opportunities there were at the French court for
changes of dress. Marie Antoinette's clothes

had to be stage-managed so that the correct colours and accessories were
matched, and a dress for a gala occasion was worn but once; every day the Queen

was presented with a book of samples of dress materials, from which she marked with a pin those she needed for the various functions of the day . . . The book was then taken back to the wardrobe and all that was needed for the day was brought in large baskets covered in silk.

As her dependence on Rose Bertin increased, the Queen gradually abandoned the public levée, since the modiste, as a commoner, was unable to attend. The Queen, valuing her milliner's advice above protocol, took to dressing, with Bertin present, in her private closet – an unprecedented insult to the women of the court.

Few couturiers and no milliners have subsequently had such power. Even as an arbiter of taste, Bertin is unique in millinery history. It is not until the 1930s and 1940s in Paris and New York that a designer with comparable influence can be found. For most of the nineteenth and early twentieth centuries, milliners were modest and their praises sung briefly, if at all.

And yet millinery establishments were patronized by all the fashionable classes. In London, for example, Gorringes, the department store founded in 1864 as a general drapers, soon became know for its speciality bonnets and trims, particularly artificial flowers and ribbons. Of milliners proper, two were especially esteemed by London shoppers. Madame Marion, 'Artiste in Artificial Flowers', was known for her flowered headdresses and caps, which won her a prize at the Crystal Palace Exhibition. Next door to her in the fashionable Burlington Arcade was Madame Parsons, famous for her 'guinea bonnets', which incorporated ideas she had picked up in Paris. Each season Parsons visited the French capital to sniff the air and see in which direction the 'ton' was moving for the next six months. In this, she was no different from many later milliners both in England and in the United States who felt that even if they did not need the inspiration of Paris, they could always benefit from the credibility such a trip could bring.

Every six months the *Millinery Trade Review*, the New York monthly, was full of advertisements parading the French connection. S. Zeimer and Feldsten of 494 Broadway announced that they were 'receiving the latest Paris novelties in flowers and fancy feathers by every steamer'. E. Lewis of 64 West Fourth Street boasted that his 'black and colour ostrich plumes and tips' were finished 'after the best Paris style' and, were a need to arise 'for rich high-cost Paris fancies', he was prepared 'with material and expert hands to meet it'. By the 1890s most of New York's top milliners were importing. Joseph Bernhard, on Broadway, dealt with the best milliners in Paris, including Madames Josse, Eugénie and Camille, as well as with Madame Virot, the most famous of all, who worked closely with Worth. Despite the superiority generally conceded to Paris milliners, there were still some independent spirits, such as Madame Marguerite Reed of East Fourteenth Street who advertised the fact that she 'takes much more pride in the work produced in her house than in importations'.

It must be remembered that for vast numbers of middle-class women in the nineteenth century a trip to the milliner was merely the start of a creative process. After buying a basic shape and purchasing the trimmings, they then proceeded to trim the hat for themselves. Last year's hat or bonnet could also be given new life by adding to, subtracting from or completely renewing the trim. Ideas were supplied by subscription magazines such as *Heideloff's Gallery of Fashion* and the *Lady's Magazine*, in Britain; the *Young Ladies Journal* and *Godey's Ladies Book* in the

Trimmed and untrimmed hats for Spring/Summer 1891, from the Jordan, Marsh and Company catalogue, Boston.

United States, the *Moniteur de la mode* and the *Journal des dames et des modes* in France, *Wiener Moden-Spiegel* in Vienna and *Eberhardts Moden Album* in Berlin. Raw materials were obtained through retail and wholesale shops in the major cities. London, for example, catered in 1817 for what the *Hatters' Gazette* referred to as every 'whim-wham and fribble-frabble' of fashion: in Oxford Street alone there were ten straw hat manufactories (where the goods were made on the premises); six bonnet warehouses (where they were not); one ribbon warehouse; three plumassiers and three fancy trimmings and fringes manufactories.

Although hat-trimming was pre-eminently a middle-class occupation, it went higher and lower than that. Jean Worth recalled in *The Well Dressed Woman* that 'Queen Alexandra could and often does trim her own hats and bonnets and makes root and branch alterations to even the most recherché Paris millinery.' Earlier, that most austere of royal ladies, Queen Victoria, encouraged the ladies of the royal household to modernize their bonnets by retrimming them. It was a policy entirely in keeping with the frugality of a monarch who, as her bonnets grew old, refused to throw them away and sent them back to the makers for repairs.

On a lower social scale, as late as the first decades of the twentieth century, trimming was still an occupation for winter evenings around the kitchen table. In *Cider with Rosie*, the poet Laurie Lee's account of his childhood in Gloucestershire, he recalls how 'we drew together round the evening lamp, the vast and easy time...' and his older sisters occupied themselves: 'Marjorie began to trim a new hat, Dorothy to write a love letter...' In the days when no woman of any class could be seen without a hat except in the most intimate of situations, ringing the changes on a very small income required ingenuity, effort and time. And trimming was not always easy or enjoyable work: the skilled hands of the milliner's workroom were rarely matched at the kitchen table.

In the 1920s an indispensable little book was published called *Millinery, How to Judge and Buy*. Written by 'Laurette', it was crammed with handy hints for shoppers who wanted style without expense. A description of one well-stocked shop suggests the scale of millinery available at the time:

> Two main classes strike the eye: the trimmed article with a view to effect; and the bare shapes, which are massed in profusion. Glass cases and cupboards hold high priced treasures, deep drawers are filled with the cheaper lines of stock, and shallow glass-protected shelves contain flowers, feathers, ribbons, bows and ornaments.

Even the least fashionable woman would expect to buy up to four new hats per season, and a 'smart dresser' might carry off fifteen or more. Fashion 'tips' and rules proliferated. Milliners pontificated on every aspect of the subject: 'Today no wardrobe is complete unless it contains at least one black velvet hat'; '...inferior silk is rarely satisfactory and cheap satin an abomination'; '...feathers are surely more suitable for wear in winter than summer'; 'It is of the *utmost* importance that a lady see herself full-length in a mirror before choosing a hat.' But behind all the condescension lay a great deal of sound information – 'A stiff silk, such as glacé, is more likely to crack or split than the soft qualities like Surah, Pongee, Tussore or Japanese' – and much instruction in the rules of taste: 'A hat should belong to the wearer as though part of herself, increasing her good looks, rather than appearing as though it were worn for its merits as a show article of millinery.'

A woman was constantly to bear in mind that 'the hat is to the rest of the attire what the coping stone is to a building – a crowning effect'. Socially, it was 'invaluable as an introduction; there is so much character to be read from its poise, adjustment, line and colouring' – and, in the 1920s, when manufacturing had returned to normal after the upheavals of World War I, there was so much choice. To ensure that the hat was 'suitable for the occasion, whether for morning or evening wear, for sport or for an afternoon call, for a quiet walk, a garden party or a private show in an art gallery' was not always an easy task. There was a confusing abundance of materials, each more or less 'suitable' for a particular occasion and a certain age: 'New fabrics are constantly being called into requisition for the purpose of hat-making, such as velour, chiffon, net, crepe de chine, tulle, georgette, lace, mousseline de soie . . . down to less ornamental . . . linen hats, duck, holland and even waterproof varieties, including leather, mackintosh and oiled silk . . .' Types and qualities of straw hats varied according to price and place of origin, and included Dunstable, Java, Luton, crinoline, Tuscan, rustic, Tagel, Yadda and satin straws. The three main types of velvet used for hats were silk-back (the most expensive, using only the silk pile); patent-back (a silk cotton); and cotton-back (the cheapest, in which only the pile warp was silk).

Hat foundations were made either of buckram – coarse, open-weave cotton fabric stiffened with size – or of the better quality and more expensive Espartra – esparto grass stretched and pressed on thick, heavily starched white muslin. For soft, tam-o'-shanter styles (the only hat named after a poem), semi-transparent book muslin was used. Linings were normally of sarsenet, a thin silk. The final effect was achieved by feathers plucked from virtually every known bird, ranging from the exotic, such as the ostrich, heron, peacock and bird of paradise, to the mundane, including the pigeon, goose, turkey and common or garden fowl, known in the trade as 'coque'. Artificial flowers were made of silk, velvet, cotton, muslin and tulle, and there were even experiments with paper ribbon, celluloid and plaster. Both customer and milliner knew that, as 'Laurette' pointed out, 'It is, in ninety-nine cases out of a hundred, the trimming that makes the hat . . .'

Up to the 1950s, millinery establishments were a strong presence on the streets of all cities and most major towns. In addition, high quality department stores carried their own millinery lines, designed and made on the premises. It is true to say that if the fashion hegemony of Paris was ever seriously challenged it was challenged through millinery. Despite the great modistes of the City of Fashion, a convincing case can be made for New York as the world's leading millinery city from the late 1930s up to the 1950s, with designers such as Lilly Daché and Mr John often outstripping the Parisians in wit, daring and style.

That this was so was the result of the same phenomenon that gave store millinery its strength – the influx of the hundreds of thousands of European refugees who crossed the Atlantic in the first decades of the twentieth century. Faced with an alien tongue, they could find work only with their hands. Hundreds of intelligent, creative women took to millinery – a skill that bypassed the language barrier. Lilly Daché herself, though not a refugee, arrived in New York and got a job at Macy's selling hats despite the fact that she could not, initially, write out the slip in English. By such means America benefited from the traditional skills and abilities of a highly developed European folk culture and no trade owed more to the refugees than that of millinery – at one time more than a third of the millinery workforce at Saks Fifth

Avenue was Russian. Theirs were the fingers – and the imaginations – that gave New York millinery such style.

Apart from Saks, the stores best known for their millinery were Henri Bendel and Bergdorf Goodman. All three ran large millinery workrooms – Saks employed forty milliners and Bergdorf as many as sixty at peak times – producing hats for their custom-made and ready-to-wear departments. Although stores bought designs in Paris and elsewhere, their millinery departments were largely autonomous. They were run by women who understood the world in which their clients moved. Miss Jessica of Henri Bendel, who in the 1950s was chief milliner at Bergdorf, was on the Social Register and understood exactly the needs of the carriage trade. Tatania, a Russian emigrée who married Alexander Lieberman, art editor of American *Vogue*, was in charge of model hats at Saks for many years. She was not a milliner, but was known for her ideas, taste, and stylish sense of colour. Like Miss Jessica, she was also valued for her social contacts. The two went to Paris for ideas but were conscious at all times that a good milliner must interpret the spirit of the house or store. A woman who patronized Bendel, for example, did so because she knew that when she walked up Fifth Avenue everyone would recognize her hat as a Bendel hat – the 'Bendel bonnet', which Cole Porter had decreed was 'the top'. The women who valued hats sufficiently to pay high prices for them were not just elegant – they were intelligent and sophisticated enough to appreciate the highest levels of creativity and workmanship.

The connection between couture and millinery goes back to Worth and his cooperation in the 1890s with Madame Virot. Virot worked closely with the couturier but interpreted his ideas in her own way – she was, after all, a grand milliner, not a mere midinette. Worth was not alone among couturiers in wishing to have his ideas creatively realized by someone trained in the demanding discipline of the milliner's art. A good milliner could interpret the spirit of a collection without sacrificing her own creative pysche and many were happy to do so. Though their contribution was officially unacknowledged, everyone in the closed fashion world of Paris knew which milliners had created the models that were paraded before customers as an essential ingredient of the couturier's line.

Paul Poiret relied on his wife to interpret his ideas for hats. Denise Poiret was her husband's muse and by far his best model, but it is for his hats that she should be remembered. It was she who actually took Poiret's idea for the tightly swathed turban with the tall aigrette and made it a reality. It became his millinery trade mark. During the 1920s, Poiret employed a former pupil from his Ecole Martine, Madeleine Panizon, to interpret his hats. Together with Alice Natter, also a former pupil, she made all Poiret's hats between 1920 and 1928. Panizon was a milliner in her own right and ran an independent business from rue de Ponthieu.

Panizon was one of many fine milliners whose names are almost totally forgotten today but who played an important role in fashion. Women like the Legroux sisters had an influence far beyond the confines of their establishment in rue Cambon in Paris. Germaine Legroux made frequent trips to the United States in the thirties, taking with her the latest styles to sell to her American clients. Equally as important were Albouy, who continued working throughout the years of World War II, and Madame Blanchot, who was honoured by being elected President of the Chambre Syndicale de la Mode Parisienne. They all worked closely with the couturiers of

Turban by Paul Poiret, 1924.

their day, who perfectly understood the importance of good millinery – many of them had actually started their working lives in millinery establishments.

'Coco' Chanel, for example, began as a milliner before moving into couture. She had always made her own clothes and hats, including straw boaters which she wore to the races. The courtesan Emilienne d'Alençon was so impressed that she adopted the boater as her signature hat. But making hats for friends was not enough to satisfy Chanel. She determined to use them to make her name and give her independence. Her English lover, Boy Capel, had the foresight to back her in her own millinery establishment and she opened Chanel Modes at 21 rue Cambon in 1910. Within two years her hats were chosen to accompany the designs of one of Paris's greatest couturiers, Jacques Doucet, for the actress Gabrielle Dorziat in Nozière's stage adaptation of Maupassant's *Bel Ami*. Chanel's hats caused a sensation. Orders poured in, including some from the high-profile diva Geneviève Vix. Even in 1914, when she opened her first boutique in Deauville, Chanel was still known almost exclusively as a milliner. Her hats, like her clothes, were far in advance of their time, unusual in their confident purity of line and lack of unnecessary decoration. As the cartoonist Sem wrote in *L'Illustration* in 1914, most milliners omitted nothing and transformed nothing: 'Flower pots, lampshades, casseroles, every conceivable kind of lid; they tried everything.'

Such an approach was anathema to Chanel, but not to the woman who many years later was to be her greatest rival. The Italian-born couturier Elsa Schiaparelli loved to shock and adored the paradoxes of the Surrealists. She understood hats and used them as an exclamation mark, a piece of fou that topped off her look and created a talking point. A Schiaparelli hat was not meant to give a woman style or enhance her elegance: Schiaparelli assumed her customers already possessed both. It was meant

Above left Gabrielle ('Coco') Chanel, wearing one of her own hat designs, 1910. *Above* Caricature, by Sem, of Chanel with her lover, Boy Capel, 1913.

Two designs by Schiaparelli. *Top* 1940s; *bottom* The 'Inkpot hat' of 1938, drawn by Marcel Vertès.

to make people sit up and take notice. The concept of outrageousness had entered twentieth-century millinery.

In the hands of Schiaparelli, Mr John, Lilly Daché and Aage Thaarup (the Danish milliner working in London who was as much in love with Surrealism as Schiaparelli herself) the outré hat was a marvellously witty addition to the vocabulary of millinery – but in hands less skilful it frequently dwindled into grotesquery of both scale and trim, making its wearer look the ridiculous victim of the milliner's misguided humour. Even at their most outrageous, Schiaparelli's hats never made women appear foolish. They were far too amusing and sophisticated for that. In fact, a woman wearing one of Schiaparelli's creations proclaimed her self-confidence while at the same time advertising the fact that she was *au fait* with the latest developments not only in fashion but also in the arts.

It was Schiaparelli's 'mad cap' of 1930 that first brought her millinery to public notice. A petite knitted tube that could be formed into any shape by the wearer, it was the chic, modern version of the Phrygian cap. Worn by Ina Claire, the American actress, it caused a sensation – and was photographed, copied and worn everywhere for years to come. Hats became a highlight of Schiaparelli's shows. Working with Salvador Dali and other Surrealist friends, she produced tiny hats – the smallest in history; huge hats – 'worn far ahead of yourself', as she put it; nose-diving hats, and even a hat decorated with a hatstand covered in miniature hats. Her shoe hat, pin-cushion hat, mutton chop hat and television hat brought her huge publicity. Throughout the 1930s, newsreels regularly featured her latest concoctions. Cinemagoers were entertained, her fellow couturiers less so – she was given more coverage than any of them. Behind all of the fun, Schiaparelli was a serious creator, which is why even her most far-fetched ideas always worked as millinery and were not merely attention-grabbing showpieces. She understood the essential balance between clothes and millinery without which no hat can be successful.

Most couturiers are able to create hats that complement their line because they do not see them as a separate entity but as an essential part of an overall look. The importance of the hat in getting the look right is aptly demonstrated by an eyewitness account quoted in Christian Dior's autobiography, *Dior by Dior*, of that point during a final dress rehearsal when Dior decided which models to show and how to accessorize them. Although Dior's millinery was created by Maud Roses, the couturier himself made the final choice. He understood hats well, having once sold them for the milliner Agnès. The eyewitness recalls the calm and dignified process:

Christian Dior hat, 1950s.

> At last, a tall boy in an overall lifted the white veil and announced, 'Un modèle, Monsieur.'
>
> As if in response, another voice declaimed the words, 'San Francisco'.
>
> And a mannequin appeared. She advanced, walked round the room with that elegant, balanced movement so completely different from a soldier's march-past, and came to a standstill . . . Christian Dior said softly, 'It needs a different hat. Something altogether more important. Now what exactly, I wonder?'
>
> Now that my attention had been directed towards it, I found that I had not even noticed before that there was a hat.

The observer goes on to describe how a hat was more or less improvised on the mannequin's head:

But it was still not good enough. From his seat, Christian Dior observed: 'It should be still more striking. Add the flower . . .'

Finally, Dior himself stood up, patted the vast edifice, moved the pins, transformed the whole thing and returned to his seat, murmuring, 'There, now that looks very pretty. Please stick in two large jet hat pins.'

As the rehearsal continues, odd snatches of conversation make it clear that the hats are not merely a decorative afterthought but are central to the fashion statement:

'The hat is not quite sensational enough. Add a mass of black veiling . . .' Dior tells an assistant who is curving the crown of a hat, 'No, leave it as it is . . .' 'That one is too formal. Double the veiling . . .' Dior explains politely, 'It is not so much a question of the hat itself, but the proportions of the whole outfit . . .'

Hat by Camille Roger, 1920s.

The master of proportion and scale was Cristobal Balenciaga. He personally designed all the hats that appeared in his collections, though he left the overseeing of the millinery workroom to his partner, Vladzio d'Attainville. The maestro himself, known affectionately to his midinettes as 'Baba', visited the millinery workroom only occasionally, but its première, Madame Janine, always showed him each hat as it was being made, for his personal approval.

Fourteen girls were employed on millinery. Each was skilled in the entire hatmaking process, but each had her own speciality. The process began when the workroom received Balenciaga's sketches. Madame Janine and d'Attainville would then begin to organize the materials and trimmings. The hat shape would be checked by Balenciaga against the dress for which it was meant and, once approved, could then be finished. For an average collection about sixty hats were produced, entirely hand-sewn.

Hat by Suzanne Talbot, 1930s.

Balenciaga loved extremes of scale. His hats were either tiny or enormous. Although he liked to enliven a collection with one or two bizarre hats, these were never vulgar. They were created to dramatize a particular dress and were not for sale – though they were, inevitably, the ones most frequently photographed. He was the first couturier to make hats from patent leather, where the leather had to be stretched and sewn by hand without leaving a wrinkle. The women buying Balenciaga hats expected them to show much careful handwork. Balenciaga trusted his customers to realize that a hat and dress were one statement and that his clothes should not be worn with a hat that had not been designed for them, as this destroyed the purity of his vision. Balenciaga was severe – as were his clothes – and he was concerned only with perfecting his creations. The women wearing them mattered not a bit. He once tried a hat on an overwhelmed and embarrassed midinette. When she protested, his reply was characteristic: 'You have a head. That is all that matters.'

Although couturiers were a powerful influence on millinery from the 1930s to the 1950s, they were catering to the most exclusive and tiny group of women. Most women of fashion bought their hats from their milliner. There were literally thousands of milliners in Paris, London and New York and their chic little shops were found on every fashionable street. In Paris, for example, Jane Blanchot, who began her millinery firm in 1923 after working as a sculptor, traded from 11 rue du Faubourg Saint-Honoré for almost fifty years. Agnès was to be found at No. 83 on the same street. The firm of Suzanne Talbot, in avenue Matignon, originally founded by Madame Tachard in 1907 but sold in 1917 to Mademoiselle Lévi, remained in business until 1956. Rose Valois was in rue Royale and Camille Roger in rue de la Paix.

One of the most important hat establishments in Paris was Maison Michel. Here hats were made, displayed and sold to prestigious wholesale or millinery clients from Germany, England and North America. Fashion shows featured the hats of all the great milliners, and clients bought the right to copy them in their own countries, at a considerable saving on the price of the original. In New York in the 1930s, an original Agnès could sell for more than 50 dollars but an identical copy, made in the United States, could be found for less than 15 dollars. The same was true of London, Berlin and most European capitals.

Paris produced male milliners of high calibre, such as Erik, Svend (who worked with Fath, Heim and Griffe) and even the shoemaker Roger Vivier who, in partnership with Suzanne Rémi, ran a boutique called Suzanne et Roger on Madison Avenue during World War II, but French millinery was overwhelmingly a female affair. It was women of the calibre of Caroline Reboux, Rose Valois, Paulette and Claude Saint-Cyr who made Paris millinery famous.

Caroline Reboux began in the classic nineteenth-century manner. Obscure and poor, she lived and worked in a tiny garret in rue de Choiseul until, in 1885, while still very young, she was discovered by two of the greatest names in fashion at the time. The Princess Metternich was the type of woman who knew how to search out the best; she had already discovered Worth. Along with the Countess of Pourtales, known as the greatest Parisian beauty of her day, she made Reboux famous. Following up rumours of a new talent, they sought her out and, as the story goes, found her working on a hat, modelling it on her knee because she could not afford a hatter's block. They immediately commissioned bonnets to wear at a charity bazaar at which the Empress Eugénie was to be present. Their hats caused a huge stir; the Empress summoned Reboux and her reputation was made. She established herself in the rue de la Paix and every fashionable woman came to see her. She dominated millinery from the 1890s until well into the 1930s, by which time the running of the business was in the hands of Lucien Rabatet, who was as brilliant a milliner as her predecessor.

Madame Lucien was famed for the sculptural quality of the hats she created and modelled on the heads of her most important customers. The English magazine *Night and Day* contains a description of Reboux's salon under Madame Lucien which, beneath the irony, vividly recaptures the mood of Paris in the 1930s, when hats were such an important part of fashion. 'Reboux has shown her collection "pour la Parisienne",' reporter Winifred Boulter wrote on 7 October 1937,

This means that the Paris season is officially open . . . Reboux used to occupy palatial showrooms on the Place de l'Opéra . . . now her windows overlook the Rond-Point des Champs Elysées . . . one goes up in a lift and walks along a circular gallery with rich red carpet, into a great room laid out . . . with quantities of triple mirrors, but no sunflower stalks. The hats are all kept in an anteroom so that they shall be untouched by profane hands.

Lucien of Reboux is a famous Paris figure. To have your hat fitted by her means you are supremely chic. To be seen walking across the showroom with Lucien's arm lightly laid round your waist means that you almost amount to

Hat by Caroline Reboux, 1936, drawn by René Gruau.

Above left Hat by Claude Saint-Cyr; *above* Turban by Paulette, 1940s.

royalty in the realm of fashion. Women have been known to wait for hours, just to get her opinion on the type of hat that will suit them.

To see a Parisienne choosing hats is a lesson. An appointment is made. A table with triple mirror is reserved. Lucien, for the elect, a saleswoman for the world in general, arrives with a satellite who carries a basket of models. One after the other is tried on and borne away. Five, six or seven are chosen. For the Parisienne orders for the season when she has chosen her frocks, and comes in for one or two more when a special occasion arises.

If you are very chic, Lucien may design a hat specially for you on your own head. Nobody just buys a hat. Each order is built and modelled on the head of the woman who is to wear it. She comes back for at least two fittings, usually devoting three whole afternoons to the collection of her season's supply . . . Millinery is a great art.

Paulette was second only to Reboux. Born in 1900 and educated in a convent school in La Tour and then in Switzerland, she began work as a model and saleswoman at the house of Lewis, which, in the years after World War I, was as important in millinery as Reboux. Paulette opened her first tiny establishment under her married name of Paulette Marchand in 1921 but it was not until 1939 that she created her famous house, Paulette-Modes, in the avenue Victor-Emmanuel. She worked in Paris throughout the war, creating all the hats for Robert Piguet's collections. It was not just the French who appreciated her hats – she had more wealthy South American clients than any other milliner in Paris.

Paulette's fame rested on her turbans. Legend has it that she made herself an impromptu hat by winding a scarf around her head and securing it with gold pins, but reality is likely to be more prosaic. The shape was classic, but the high drape that pulled the turban back off the face and gave it height at the back was new. Queues quickly formed outside Paulette's shop in avenue Franklin D. Roosevelt, so determined were stylish women to be seen in the latest addition to the vocabulary of chic. The turban and Paulette were linked from then on. When, in 1946, the milliner was invited to the United States by Carmel Snow, editor of *Harper's Bazaar*, journalists who were expecting her to wear the latest turban were appalled when she appeared hatless. 'Pastry cooks don't always eat cakes,' was her response.

Paulette made hats for every chic woman who passed through Paris, including Gloria Swanson, Garbo, Dietrich, Edith Piaf and even Schiaparelli. In 1972 she made the Duchess of Windsor's hat for the funeral of the Duke and was for many years the official milliner to Madame Pompidou and Madame Giscard d'Estaing. In 1974 she received the Legion of Honour. Her work with couturiers spanned the period from 1941, when she first started with Piguet, to her death in 1984, when she was still designing for Claude Montana. In between, she was milliner for Chanel, Cardin, Ungaro, Thierry Mugler and Guy Laroche. Through them, her influence was immense.

Claude Saint-Cyr served her apprenticeship with the milliner Rose Descat and the couturier Patou before opening her own establishment in 1937 under the pseudonym by which she is always known. Her success was instant and can be measured by the fact that she began with five employees and by the end of her first year had added another seventy. Her clients came from the top echelons of international society and included the Duchess of Windsor and Lady Mountbatten. When the war interrupted her business, she moved to the South of France but, after the Armistice, opened again in Paris. A businesswoman as well as a creator, she started a branch in London in the 1950s and, under the guidance of Norman Hartnell, became one of the Queen's milliners. The degree of Saint-Cyr's integrity as a milliner is reflected in her comment that 'for a dress the measurements are very important, but for a hat they must be correct to a millimetre. A little too far forward, a little too far back and it's finished. It no longer flatters the face.'

Although a Paris bonnet was considered the last word in chic in the 1930s, French milliners had neither a monopoly of talent nor of influence. Without smart society, millinery becomes nothing; without an efficiently organized social world where standards of dress are pre-eminent considerations, a hat becomes merely a headcovering. In the twentieth century both these prerequisites for the smart life were much stronger in London and New York than in Paris. The period from the 1930s to the 1950s was transitional for fashion; it saw the lingua franca of style cease to be exclusively French. The common tongue of English, the United States dollar and the social clout of Great Britain and its Season, sponsored by royalty: all conspired to weaken the power of Paris.

This did not stop milliners flocking to the French capital in the 1930s and shipping back on the *Queen Mary*, the *Normandie* or the *Europa* boxfuls of hats from which they would develop their own lines in the coming season. They continued to do this after Paris had re-established itself in 1947, sending back their treasures on Pan Am clippers and on the Orient Express. By this time, however, London and New York had their own healthy millinery businesses and these shipments serviced only a specialist trade.

Aage Thaarup was at the centre of London millinery. Like Schiaparelli, he thrived on publicity and his constant flow of witty ideas for hats – plus their exposure through newspaper and newsreel coverage – made him the most famous milliner of the 1930s. He was given more media attention than other milliners not only because his Surrealist creations had a whimsy that rivalled anything in Paris but also because he was milliner to Queen Elizabeth. In a society based on the hierarchy of royalty and title, the benefits of such a connection are incalculable. Everywhere the Queen went she was photographed and in the accompanying copy Thaarup's name was mentioned. This being said, Thaarup was the only milliner in London whose talent matched those of his counterparts in Paris and it was this fact that ultimately made his reputation.

According to Thaarup, George VI took a great interest in his wife's clothes, including her hats, and was as open to ideas as his father, George V, had been closed. The latter refused to allow Queen Mary to follow fashion and objected to any change in her manner of dress, which probably explains why she wore the same high toques for more than forty years. These were, in fact, satisfactory crown substitutes and helped give the Queen a stately aura that prompted the diarist Henry 'Chips' Channon to report that meeting her was 'like talking to St Paul's Cathedral'. Her toques arrived from her milliner complete with a sewn-on 'bang' of false hair, so that hat and hair were ready to wear without the attentions of a hairdresser.

George VI, by contrast, encouraged Queen Elizabeth to experiment. He was the inspiration behind Hartnell's Winterhalter look, a style that became an icon of twentieth-century royal dressing. He was delighted with Thaarup's fantasies, even with the hat trimmed with tiny plastic vegetables which the milliner created for the Queen when she was Duchess of York. At its unveiling the future king roared with laughter. 'You're mad!' he cried, but he insisted that his wife buy it.

Thaarup had joined the charmed circle of suppliers to the royal family on the recommendation of Lady Doris Vyner. It was a bold move on her part. Up to this point, royal dressing had been remarkable for the fact that it was essentially unfashionable. Queen Mary had turned her back on any new developments and Queen Elizabeth had not yet found her true style – which allowed the Duchess of Windsor to joke that the best thing the Queen could do to promote British fashion was to stay at home. Thaarup was a very fashionable milliner indeed. He was also clever. He knew that by lending hats to socialites who lunched at the Berkeley Buttery – *the* place to be seen in mid-thirties London – he would soon have the whole town talking and a high proportion of its chicest women flocking to his tiny shop to buy the latest novelty. As a publicist, he was a true descendant of Rose Bertin. But, behind all the showmanship, there was a craftsman who had learned his trade. Thaarup was aware that the essence of a good hat is flattery and that observers must look at the woman before they notice the hat. To achieve such a response and still produce a 'newsworthy' hat is the hardest balancing act in fashion.

Thaarup's approach began long before he sat his customer down in front of the triple mirror to try on shapes. Every new client had to walk across the salon, hatless, while he observed how she moved and noted the width of her hips, which he considered the key 'balance point' against which a hat should be correctly proportioned and scaled. He was a perfectionist, and to ensure that his hats were properly worn, he made his customers practice putting them on in front of him. A line inside the hat showed how it was to be aligned in relation to the nose.

New York society figures of the thirties and forties were dressed by Hattie Carnegie, who bought clothes from Paris as well as employing her own designers. She was the first American designer to wield power equal to that of the French. Born in Vienna in 1889, her real name was Henrietta Kanengeiser but when the family emigrated it was changed to Carnegie. After the early death of her father, Carnegie was forced to look for work, and started her career as a cashier at Macy's department store. By the age of fifteen she was trimming hats in the millinery department. In 1909, not yet twenty, she opened up her own shop on East Tenth Street in conjunction with a friend, Rose Roth, who made dresses. It was called 'Carnegie – Ladies' Hatter'. By 1913 they were able to move to West Eighty-sixth Street, with a capital of 100,000 dollars behind them. Carnegie eventually bought out her partner and founded Hattie Carnegie Inc.

Carnegie's importance in giving Americans confidence in their indigenous talent was enormous. It was from her that America's true fashion sprang. During the 1940s she was employing more than one thousand people to produce her clothes, hats, perfumes and accessories. Her hats bore the label 'Hatnegie' and were sold coast to coast in top quality stores. After her death in 1956, the business that had relied on her flair slowly faded away.

Lilly Daché, a European like Carnegie, was born in Beigles, France, the daughter of a farmer. She worked briefly at Suzanne Talbot and was a midinette at Reboux for four years. She arrived in New York in 1924 with 15 dollars in her purse. After a short time, she managed to find a job selling hats at Macy's but her English was so poor that she was dismissed. She then found work with what she subsequently described as a 'hole-in-the-wall' milliner at Seventy-seventh street and Broadway. Out of her pay of 25 dollars per week, she saved 15 dollars and, after ten weeks, bought out her employer. Daché had no capital and was forced to ask her first customers to pay a deposit to enable her to buy material. Recognizing her flair, they did so and she was soon running with a turnover of more than forty hats a day. Daché and Carnegie were remarkably similar: neither was a technician; they had little grasp of practical hatmaking techniques; both were tough, strong women with dramatic personalities; each was a businesswoman to the tip of her fingers – and they both became very rich.

In 1946 Daché published her autobiography, *Talking Through My Hats*. It was high on opinion and low on fact, but her name was so big that it became a bestseller. Like Rose Bertin, she knew how to keep her name in the limelight by reflecting what was current: in 1940, to commemorate the Fall of Paris, she created an all black collection. A rival milliner once said of Daché: 'She was making Fords, while I was making Cadillacs.' It was unfair, but it typified the jealousy provoked by the woman who had made herself *the* American milliner in the eyes of the world. Always on the lookout for good designers prepared to work anonymously, Daché discovered Halston in Chicago and brought him to New York. Her theatrical flair and showmanship were at times dangerously close to vulgarity but they ensured that she was patronized by all the movie stars of the thirties and forties. Arriving after Daché had wound up her business in 1968, Loretta Young bought thirty hats: all that remained of the output of America's most famous woman milliner.

Lilly Daché died in 1989 but her contemporary, Mr John, outlived her. Unlike Hattie Carnegie and Daché, he was a practical and practising milliner. He was also one of New York's great entertainers, adored by his customers for his outrageous behaviour. A fashion dictator, he liked to emphasize his importance by dressing like Napoleon and sporting a Napoleonic hairstyle. Mr John's full name is John Piocelle and he claims to have been born in Florence, though he is listed in the Celebrity Register as Hans Harburger, born in Munich in 1906. Like his friend Diana Vreeland, Mr John has several versions of the major events in his life. What is certain is that every star from Mary Pickford to Marilyn Monroe and every fashionable woman from Mrs Otis (of Otis Elevators fame) to Mrs William Paley have been his customers.

Before World War II, Mr John was in partnership with Frederic Hirst in a business known as John Frederics. In the 1950s he set up under his own name on West Fifty-seventh Street in surroundings of perverse grandeur. His press release sets the tone:

> Sweeping white and gold doors form an entrance into the seventy-foot custom fashion salon decorated in white, gold, crystal and mirrored Louis XVI decor where a life-sized white Bisque cupid with paired doves and blackamoors dressed in gold and jewels stand guard. Lighted with a flourish of four large bronze d'ore and paired candlelit cut crystal girandoles . . . counter-reflected in mirrored arches on the opposite wall as in the Galerie des Glaces at Versailles . . .

In addition, Mr John owned a life-size ceramic leopard with a diamanté collar, a lion in a scarlet garden party hat and, to top it all, a live pink parrot called Paris, which was allowed the freedom of the salon. Despite such vulgarity, Mr John produced hats that were exuberant, witty and stylish without ever being crude. Behind all the posturing was a great milliner.

Mr John designed two of the most romantic hats of this century – for Scarlett O'Hara in the film *Gone with the Wind*. The leghorn cartwheel with the deep green velvet ribbons summed up the eighteenth-century elegance of plantation life just as the bonnet that Rhett Butler brought from Paris to persuade the widowed Scarlett to give up her hypocritical mourning betokened everything the French capital stood for. Made of 'dark-green taffeta, lined with watered silk of a pale jade colour', it made Scarlett cry 'Oh, the darling thing!' and Mr John claims to have been paid 20,000 dollars for it. As he wrote later, Vivien Leigh and David O. Selznick offered no advice. All the actress said was, 'John, all I ask is, let them see me before they see the hats.' He claimed that this was the philosophy behind all his designs – to

Mr John's salon, New York.

complement rather than overwhelm the wearer. Mr John was no stranger to Hollywood, having worked for many years with the designer Adrian. He advised Cecil Beaton on the hats for *My Fair Lady* and, years before, had served a theatrical apprenticeship providing headgear for revues at the Casino de Paris and Folies Bergère, working with Mistinguett and Cécile Sorel.

Although John's craving for publicity often involved outrageous behaviour, professional commentators saw his true worth. Dorothy Hawkins, writing in the *New York Times*, pointed out that 'beneath all the fun and whimsy he is a gifted designer and skilled workman who produces some of the most original, wearable and flattering hats to be seen anywhere'. Eugenia Sheppard of the *New York Post* agreed, claiming that 'Mr John is *the* artist among milliners.' At his peak, he employed 150 people and had an annual turnover of 7 million dollars. He produced more than sixteen thousand hats a year and in one year alone his custom hats made 1.5 million dollars. John retired in the 1970s, declaring that women no longer had character or chic, having 'sold-out' to hairdressers who 'make orthopaedic hairdos and french-fried curls'. By then he had become the world's richest milliner, though he professed contempt for money and refused to discuss prices. 'I billed; they paid,' he claimed and, if they questioned, he would reply, 'Madam, do you want a hat or something to show to your husband's accountant?'

John believes that 'the true American aristocrats were international, unlike their English counterparts. They worked to a level of world taste.' It was thanks to them that the American millinery industry achieved such success. Milliners like Sally Victor aimed at the standard they set and determined to make fine hats affordable to the vast majority of middle-class American women. She succeeded and, in so doing, made her firm the biggest middle-market millinery company in the United States. John accused her of 'brain-picking', but she was unrepentant, telling the *Saturday Evening Post*, 'What I pinch are marketable ideas.' Born in Sacramento, Pennsylvania, Victor studied painting in Paris before following the classic American milliners' path and working in Macy's millinery department. Between 1923 and 1930 she designed for Serge, the millinery house of Sergui Victor, whom she married. The firm took her name and, by the mid-thirties, was a considerable success. The First Lady, Mamie Eisenhower, wore a Victor hat to her husband's inauguration and Prince Rainier bought one for Grace Kelly. But it was Victor's lower priced ranges that made her wealthy – her 1950s Sally V label sold for as little as 15 dollars.

By the 1950s, however, the days when millinery and its creators were a central and vital part of the fashion world were drawing to their close. The war had made into workers vast numbers of previously leisured women who relished the freedom and independence that came with their new status. They would never again be prepared to devote so much of their time to their appearance. Hats seemed an unnecessary encumbrance as well as suggesting attitudes to femininity that were already beginning to seem outdated and inappropriate for modern life. As the sixties approached it was clear that youth and vigour left no place for the old formalities on which the continued health of the millinery world had depended. To many in the trade the future looked at best problematical and at worst bleak. Certainly, as millinery slipped into the doldrums, only the most farsighted and optimistic could have held out hope for any eventual recovery.

Wheel of Fashion, 'Les Variations de la mode et du chapeau', c. 1840.

LA MODE.

DO-IT-YOURSELF MILLINERY

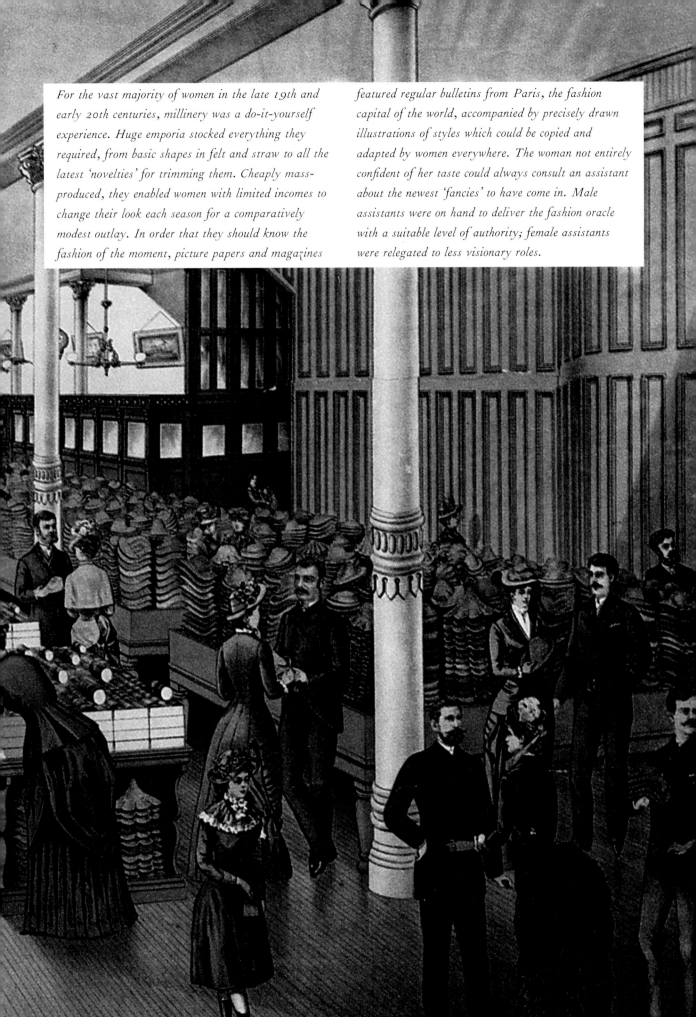

For the vast majority of women in the late 19th and early 20th centuries, millinery was a do-it-yourself experience. Huge emporia stocked everything they required, from basic shapes in felt and straw to all the latest 'novelties' for trimming them. Cheaply mass-produced, they enabled women with limited incomes to change their look each season for a comparatively modest outlay. In order that they should know the fashion of the moment, picture papers and magazines featured regular bulletins from Paris, the fashion capital of the world, accompanied by precisely drawn illustrations of styles which could be copied and adapted by women everywhere. The woman not entirely confident of her taste could always consult an assistant about the newest 'fancies' to have come in. Male assistants were on hand to deliver the fashion oracle with a suitable level of authority; female assistants were relegated to less visionary roles.

AIN SALESROOM.
564 & 566 BROADWAY. NEW YORK.

'Chez la Modiste', c. 1895

HAT SHOPS

Buying a hat is not something to be undertaken lightly.
It requires thought, consideration and professional
advice. In the days when hats were an essential part of
everyday life, there were often only a few yards
between one millinery establishment and another on the
fashionable streets of Europe and North America.

Auguste Macke, *The Hat Shop*, 1913

In order to compete, milliners had to provide a high level of service. The good milliner was expected to be familiar with the social life of her customers as well as being au fait *with the latest fashion developments in Paris. It was no use creating hats that were the 'dernier cri' if they were not suitable.*

Milliners in major cities not only made their own creations, they also frequently imported expensive French original models. Their success in a highly competitive field rested on the speed of their reaction to fashion's changes: it was essential to stock the latest novelty trims and ribbons as quickly as possible.

PAULETTE

Good design is about reduction rather than detailing. Precision of scale is especially essential for great millinery.

No milliner understood the importance of reduction and precision better than Paulette. Her hats are sublime because they have been cut back to their essence, with all unnecessary decoration stripped away to reveal a form as pure as a sculpture by Brancusi. Only when the shape was so perfect that the slightest change would destroy its scale might Paulette consider whether or not any decoration was required. On the rare occasions when it was, she spent as long in ensuring that the decoration became an integral part of the hat – and not

merely an addition – as she had on the original shape. Paulette's genius is confirmed by the fact that from the 1950s to the 1980s (a period of unprecedented change in attitudes towards fashion) she worked with the great designers and always created hats that were in tune with the mood of the moment. She was rightly known in Paris as millinery's only true intellectual.

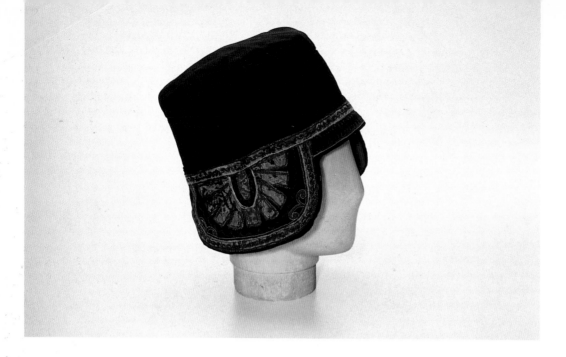

JEANNE LANVIN

The house of Lanvin was founded by Jeanne Lanvin in 1886 with a credit for 300 francs, savings of 40 francs and an iron determination to succeed. The firm was originally a millinery establishment; Lanvin had begun her working life by being apprenticed to the famous milliner Suzanne Talbot in 1880, when she was only thirteen. Even after the house of Lanvin had become one of the greatest couture houses in the world, it was always as well known for its hats as for its gowns. Farsighted and imaginative, Jeanne Lanvin approached the design of hats from a totally modern stance, turning her back on old-fashioned ideas of romantic millinery. Her hats, like her whole approach to design, were avant-garde, flattering and essentially feminine. Throughout the 1920s and 1930s, they were renowned for their chic and elegance.

Opposite, top to bottom 1915/20; 1925/
30; 1930/1935

This page, top left 1918

Top right 1919

Centre left and right 1923

Bottom left and right 1936

SCHIAPARELLI

Above Designs for the shoe hat and others, 1930s

Opposite Schiaparelli suit and hat, photographed by Horst, 1938

Elsa Schiaparelli was the madcap designer of Paris, literally and figuratively. During the 1930s her collections were famous for their originality, wit and impudence. Although many couturiers before her had been influenced by their close friendships with painters, designers and illustrators, Schiaparelli was the first to enter an artistic movement so wholeheartedly that its attitudes permeated all that she did.

Surrealism was her great love and she worked closely with artists such as Salvador Dali to produce unexpected effects. Her collaboration with Dali was most successful in the hats they produced throughout the 1930s, the most famous of which was, undoubtedly, the hat designed in the shape of a shoe.

BALENCIAGA

Touchy and difficult, Cristobal Balenciaga was the recluse of French fashion in the 1950s and 1960s. While Dior, Fath and Balmain became social figures whose lives were fodder for the gossip columnist, Balenciaga firmly closed his doors against any intrusions that might interrupt the only thing that mattered to him – the creation of perfectly beautiful clothes. He left nothing to chance, taking charge in his ateliers of every aspect of design, including the millinery that so often acted as the exclamation point to a look, highlighting and emphasizing his line. He understood the drama of opposing scales and tended to make his hats either very large or extremely small in contrast to the scale of the outfit for which they were designed. For such an austere man, his creations were often surprisingly witty – as these two classic examples show. Pert and precise, they guaranteed attention for the woman lucky enough to wear them.

Left Hat by Balenciaga, 1963

Opposite Hat by Balenciaga, photographed by David Seidner, 1986

LILLY DACHÉ

Great milliners have frequently felt that they owed it to their public to enjoy lives as fashionable and extreme as many of their creations. As this exquisitely posed publicity picture of Lilly Daché, taken in the 1940s, makes clear, the effect aimed at was a certain controlled drama – more jewelry than most of her customers would care to wear but not so much as to appear vulgar. New York milliners like Daché moved in high society, were considered friends by some of their grandest customers and lived stylish lives.

But, of course, to achieve such eminence the milliner had to have an exceptional creative talent. Lilly Daché clearly did. In her autobiography Talking Through My Hats, *she describes how, when she was a young woman just starting her career, she always wore one of her own creations when she went out to dinner. Invariably, she had sold it to a fellow diner before the meal was finished. From such beginnings she built an empire that brought her wealth, power and considerable social standing.*

Opposite Lilly Daché in her workshop, New York, 1941

Above Daché hat with veil, drawn by Marcel Vertès, 1943

Left Hat by Daché, 1961

175

Christian Dior died in 1957; eleven years later Cristobal Balenciaga closed his doors, declaring that there were no women left to dress. So an era came to an end. Formality, which had been the backbone of couture clothing, slipped out of fashion – in every sense. The new designers were more interested in ready-to-wear than in couture. They were keen to harness the technical advances in mass production to provide cheap, well-made clothes for the masses, rather than superlatively made clothes for the privileged few. The days when the lining of a dress was automatically made to the same exacting standards as the dress itself were almost over; soon, 99 percent of dresses would be made without any lining at all.

Couture reached its high point in the late 1950s, when the shock of Dior's New Look had been assimilated and the baton of fashion leadership has passed to Balenciaga and Givenchy. But it was Dior's successor, the young Yves Saint Laurent – frail of frame but robustly talented – who realized that the spirit of the age had changed. He was the first Parisian designer to understand that ready-to-wear clothes were what women and the fashion industry both wanted. Freedom from fuss and formality were the bedrock of the new approach to fashion. Informality slipped into casualness as women began to realize that the world would not collapse if they went out stockingless or appeared at work in a sleeveless dress. The late fifties and early sixties saw fashion editors, who should have been in the forefront of the new movement, stranded like dinosaurs in their chic couture clothing. Most of them still sat at their desks wearing gloves and a hat. But the rest of the world did not.

One of the first casualties of the new informality was, inevitably, the hat. For a brief period, it hovered in limbo, seen as an optional extra rather than as a fashion essential. But by the early 1960s it had received the ageist kiss of death: young women felt that hats were irrelevant to their fast-moving new freedoms and were suitable only for the stiff formality of the life of the older woman. No item of clothing can recover its former position once it has been consigned to the ghetto of middle-aged and elderly wear, and the formal hat was no exception. The few women who still allowed them in their wardrobes kept them for special occasions of the kind where conformity and custom demanded a headcovering: weddings, funerals – the sort of official or heightened occasion when the humdrum world was forgotten and a form of fancy dress prevailed.

Boy George, photographed by Nick Knight for his album *Tense, Nervous Headache*, wearing a hat made from Brazilian recycled plastic bags.

That the new attitudes symbolized an enormous shift in women's thinking is apparent if we compare the late 1930s with the early 1960s. In the thirties (as in the preceding decades) no self-respecting woman would ever be seen in a public place without a hat. This was not merely true of Fifth Avenue, Bond Street or the rue de Rivoli. It applied equally to Torquay, Tucson or Thiers. Indeed, it was the case in every small town and village in the Western world. Regardless of her class, putting on her hat before going out was as much second nature to a woman as picking up her purse. Her hat was part of her personality. But after the 'swinging sixties', the attitudes of women changed so radically that hats were, in future, always to be worn in parentheses – isolated, special, unusual.

The power of the hat, like the power of couture, was diminished by the fact that in the late fifties and early sixties the young took over as fashion leaders. Youth came swinging in with the new decade, confident and iconoclastic, determined not to be constrained by the rules that had kept their mothers in thrall. The sixties saw virtually everything that had been important in fashion for the past fifty years cheerfully jettisoned by young women bored by what they had worn last week, let alone what had been in fashion for a decade or more. They could see nothing new in hats. All the shapes, materials and trims had been fully exploited in the 1930s and every possible variation in scale and volume had been explored in the 1950s. But what *was* new and exciting was hair. Free and untrammelled or carefully coaxed and laquered, it had, the new woman argued, a flexibility not found in hats and, above all, it was *part* of her, not an extra to be popped on at the last moment. Milliners found themselves up against the ropes for the first time in over a hundred years. Even the greatest names were forced to cut back on staff and most eventually closed, killed as much by hairspray and wigs as by new attitudes.

In the sixties, professional hairdressers took over almost entirely from milliners as the creators of headdress. Not since the late eighteenth century had they wielded

Below Vidal Sassoon haircut, 1963; *below right* 1960s hairstyle.

such power. As *Life* noted in 1961, they were 'sought after, showered with gifts, lavishly entertained' – and increasingly turned to for hat substitutes. And though there would seem to be limits to the scope for change of mood or personality offered by hair, hairdressers were up to the challenge. Variety was provided by developing techniques of hair colouring into such a huge industry that an article in *Cosmopolitan* magazine in 1961 estimated that U.S. women were spending 45 million dollars in drugstores and 250 million dollars in beauty parlours on hair colouring alone. Hairdressers also capitalized on the new skill in wigmaking. For many women hairpieces became a part of their general makeup, to be carried in the purse along with lipstick, powder and perfume and pinned to their own hair for a special occasion or evening out. Complete wigs had also become a fashion item and hairdressers were perfectly happy to style them just as they would a client's hair. In 1962, *Newsweek* estimated that as many as half a million U.S. women were regularly wearing wigs as part of their fashion 'look'. They simply did not need to return to hats, with all their discomfort, inflexibility and social constraints.

However, couturiers did return. Few designers sent clothes down the catwalk without the trimming of a hat, so acknowledging that, despite changed attitudes, a finished, all-over fashion look could still not be achieved without one. This fact continues to be acknowledged today. Few outfits by Lagerfeld for Chanel, for example, are shown without hats, and even a designer as uncompromisingly radical as Claude Montana feels that his message is incomplete without them. Made especially for the show, such hats rarely, if ever, go into production because designers – hard-headed businessmen that they are – know that, no matter how delicious the creation or how essential to the effect of the clothes, hats will not be bought in numbers sufficient to cover, let alone justify, their production costs.

But hats continue to be made and millinery is still a trade, though business is minute compared to earlier times. A certain kind of woman still believes that, for

Hats by Karl Lagerfeld for Spring/Summer 1990.

truly formal occasions, no hairstyle – no matter how beautiful and complex – can take the place of a hat. The London milliner Graham Smith believes that the Royal family – at the centre of so many formal occasions – has saved British millinery, and that the New York trade has been saved by Jewish women whose society is still sufficiently structured to require the frequent wearing of a hat. As a visit to any milliner's establishment will confirm, ordinary, everyday hats, of the kind so common in the past, will no longer be found there. Their place has been taken by extravagant, elegant, larger-than-life creations clearly intended for a special occasion, be it a royal garden party or a bar mitzvah. These hats, though beautiful, have a strong sense of *déja vu*, in that they are, like couture clothing, created in a context that is essentially old-fashioned. They represent a recycling of ideas that were already fully exploited in the days when millinery was at the cutting edge of fashion creativity.

Many young milliners see their role as creating hats that are, above all, head-turning. They ignore the woman who has to wear them and the society in which she moves. To catch the attention by distorted scale or excessive and mindless decoration is as vulgar as it is unsophisticated. Good fashion, in millinery as in every other area, is about control and understatement. Hats made by a milliner who disregards his client's needs are bound to fail. They will overwhelm the wearer and destroy whatever else she has on. This is a common occurrence today, when clothes and hats are designed separately, with little understanding or consideration of how they are to interact. Modern fashion eclecticism further worsens the situation. In the past, there was a line for each season and everything, including millinery, was designed to enhance that line. A couturier's shape for that season would impose its own discipline on the milliner with whom he collaborated. Such consensus has largely disappeared and it leaves milliners – especially those with little experience – with hardly any back-up or outside control. It is a problem inherent in an area of fashion that has not kept pace with mainstream developments.

However, it is not the only problem. An equally serious difficulty lies with the client. Whereas fashionable women in the past knew how to choose a hat, most women today, like their milliners, are inclined to confuse extravagance with glamour and distortion with style. Any visitor to the Royal Enclosure at Ascot knows how very ill-at-ease most modern women are when it comes to the wearing of hats. Indeed, they could hardly be otherwise, since ease in clothing comes with daily familiarity. Clearly, a head wearing a large picture hat must be held differently from the way it is held when hatless; a woman used to walking with her hair free does not walk in the same way when her hair is confined in a hat; her neck and head gestures are equally different. That is why today's women look gauche and unnatural in hats and why their appearance often provokes astonishment or amusement.

Of course, there are still milliners who know their trade, just as there are still plenty of elegant hats being produced. But what has been lost is the balance between informed client, inspired couturier and intuitive milliner. Several couturiers began their fashion lives as milliners, just as many couturiers have always designed their own hats for a collection. It is in the work of these designers that an understanding of the interplay between hats and clothes is apparent.

The most famous example of a milliner who crossed over and became a clothes designer is Halston, known to every fashion follower as the man who took the pillbox hat designed by Adrian for Greta Garbo in the 1932 film *As You Desire Me* and reinvented it for Jackie Kennedy as America's crown substitute. The First Lady found it so flattering that it became her 'signature' hat for all her official engagements. Halston, whose full name was Roy Halston Frowick, was born in Iowa in 1932, and set himself up as a milliner in the Ambassador Hotel in Chicago in the early 1950s. There he met Lilly Daché, who persuaded him to work for her at her New York salon. Daché thought so highly of his work that she allowed him to show his own small collection of hats as an independent group within her collection. It was an immediate success and, in less than a year with Daché, Halston was named co-designer. The few skills Halston did not learn from Lilly Daché were acquired through his friendship with Charles James, one of the great experts and original fashion luminaries of the twentieth century, acknowledged by Balenciaga as 'the greatest couturier in the world'. So it was as one of America's most commercially accomplished milliners that Halston was lured from Daché to Bergdorf Goodman in 1958 to work with the legendary Jessica Daube, described by Cecil Beaton as 'The High Priestess of Millinery'. He took the place of the Cuban milliner, Adolfo, who walked out when Bergdorf Goodman refused to put his name on the labels and became a dress designer, famed in the eighties as the couturier to Nancy Reagan.

In the 1950s Bergdorf Goodman's millinery department was renowned. Every fashionable New York woman bought there, from Diana Vreeland to jet-setters such as Mrs William S. Paley, Elsa Maxwell, Mrs Paul Mellon and Mrs Douglas Fairbanks, Jr. But Halston's keenest customer was Jackie Kennedy. She returned to him regularly, not only because she admired his millinery skills but also because his head was the same size as hers and she knew that her hats would fit perfectly because he always tried them on before shipping them to her. When it came to ordering her outfit for the inauguration, the President suggested that it should come from the American designer Oleg Cassini, but his wife insisted that her hat should be made by Halston. It was a pillbox, deliberately large-scale in order to accommodate both her head and hairstyle and yet be worn comfortably pushed back. It became an instant bestseller, copied the length and breadth of the land.

Much the same thing was to happen many years later with the Princess of Wales. Her first 'signature' hats were created in the early eighties by the London milliner

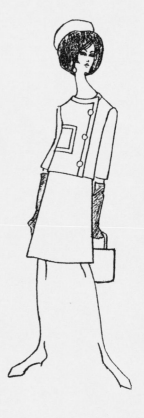

Above Jackie Kennedy in Halston suit with pillbox hat; *left* The Princess of Wales in John Boyd hat with feather trim, 1981.

John Boyd. Their small curved brims and discrete feather trim perfectly personified the middle-class need for undemonstrative clothing. Women of all ages and sizes wore what was popularly known as the 'Lady Di' hat and John Boyd's success was assured. Boyd had been introduced to the princess through her mother, Mrs Shand Kydd, who was one of the many society customers he had gathered round him since first opening his London salon in 1946. Born in Edinburgh, Boyd served an apprenticeship with the Queen Mother's milliner, Aage Thaarup: his first job was dyeing veils to match the hats and then drying them out of an upstairs window. With more than forty years as a milliner behind him, Boyd is the doyen of London milliners. He makes hats for everyone in London society, including ex-prime minister Margaret Thatcher.

Another of London's society milliners who emerged in the early 1950s was the Frenchwoman, Simone Mirman, who trained in Paris with Rose Valois and worked briefly in Schiaparelli's London branch before opening her own establishment in 1947. What was to prove a long and highly successful association with the British royal family began when Princess Margaret, who thought Thaarup's prices too high, bought from her in 1952. The Queen Mother followed and then, finally, the Queen herself. Mirman was usually asked to provide the hats to accompany outfits by Norman Hartnell just as Frederick Fox later made hats for Hardy Amies's clothes. She was in many respects the leading light of a group of London milliners working in the fifties and early sixties that included James Wedge and the entrepreneur Otto Lucas, whose label appeared on some of the most sophisticated hats of the time. In fact, Lucas did not design but bought with great skill and taste from milliners and couturiers in London and Paris, paying a license fee in order to reproduce hats from their collections as line-for-line copies sold under his own name. He was killed in an aeroplane crash when returning from such a buying trip in Paris.

Graham Smith is another London-based milliner who, like Boyd and Mirman, survived the lean sixties and uncertain seventies to come into his own in the more hat-conscious eighties and nineties. At a time when young milliners sometimes produce hats that look as if they have been made with a knife and fork, the skill, experience and knowledge of the older milliners has become much in demand. Smith makes hats for the Princess of Wales, the Duchess of York, Princess Margaret and the Duchess of Gloucester, as well as stars of the calibre of Joan Collins, Barbra Streisand and Elizabeth Taylor. Born in 1939, Smith studied fashion in London before specializing in millinery at the Royal College of Art. His postgraduate work attracted so much attention that when Paul Tuede, the milliner at Lanvin, died suddenly in 1958, Smith was asked to take his place. He worked in Paris for one year but, by his own admission, was too young to appreciate what Lanvin's customers required. However, the experience of working to the highest levels of couture has stood Smith in good stead. Although he has produced ready-to-wear lines for the middle-market mass-manufacturer Kangol for many years, it is as a model hatter that Graham Smith is known, and he admits that his style is not easy to sell at mass-market level. He understands that the essence of a good model hat is that it must suit the woman so completely as to seem part of her, never overpowering her in its scale, shape or decoration. Unlike many younger milliners, Smith knows that truly elegant hats are self-effacing.

Perfectionism is what links Smith with the young French milliner Philippe Model, a polymath designer who creates shoes and other accessories, as well as the hats for which he is famous. It is a testimony to the high level of his work that he provides the show hats for many of Paris's top designers, including Sonia Rykiel, Claude Montana, Martine Sitbon and Jean-Paul Gaultier, and includes among his private clients Catherine Deneuve, Fanny Ardant and Princess Caroline of Monaco. Model was born in Sens, one hour's train journey south of Paris, in 1956. His father owned a tannery, so it is perhaps not surprising that Model's first designs were of shoes and handbags. He studied millinery with an ex-employee of Paulette's and, later, worked briefly with Paulette herself. From the outset, Model's designs had éclat. He used strong and often discordant colours and employed original and eye-catching materials. However, as could be expected from a French milliner, his hats did not sacrifice elegance to shock effect – which is why there are more hats by Model at the Prix de Diane each year than by any other milliner. His customers claim that Model's hats sit more comfortably than those of his rivals – which may be a result of the fact that, like Halston, he fits many of them on his own head.

The London milliner Stephen Jones is a surrealist. Born one year after Model, he graduated from London's St Martin's School of Art in 1979 and began to make hats for friends. It was at the beginning of that period of creativity and outrageousness that was to make London the centre for wild and iconoclastic fashion ideas. Pop music and clubbing were at the heart of all youthful culture and they had an enormous influence on Jones. He made hats for Boy George, Spandau Ballet and Duran Duran and, by 1980, was sufficiently established to open his own shop. Stephen Jones is possibly the most original milliner working today. His hats echo Schiaparelli's from the 1930s, but are always completely up to the minute in mood. He entirely understands the zeitgeist of the times. In the Fashion Institute of Technology's huge 'Fashion and Surrealism' exhibition of 1987, Jones's hats stood out as having an artistic integrity rare in fashion, holding their own with the work of some of the greatest designers of the twentieth century.

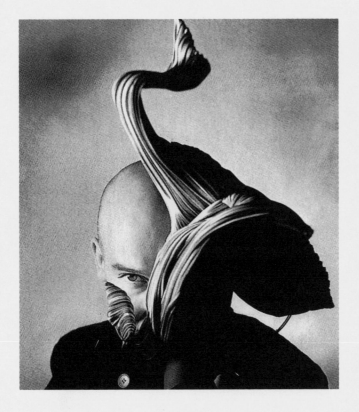

Stephen Jones with one of his hats.

Following pages

Sugar-loaf hat by Schiaparelli, drawn by Christian Bérard, *c.* 1943.

Comme des Garçons hat, photographed by Minsei Tominaga for *Six* magazine, issue 2, 1988.

PHILIPPE MODEL

Philippe Model is the cheery iconoclast of French millinery who believes that only by breaking the rules can stylish hats be created. His huge reputation in France and far beyond suggests that he may be right. Certainly, it can be guaranteed that in any smart gathering around the world – racing at Chantilly, a film star's wedding in California, a garden party in Sydney – some of the most arresting hats will have been designed by Model.

As extrovert as his creations, Model bears out the old contention that a hat with personality can only be created by a milliner with personality. Model's hats break through the barrier of conventional taste to reach glorious heights of originality, rather as his personal taste in dress does. He is the Orson Welles of the millinery world.

Top Hat designs by Philippe Model

Right Philippe Model in his marquee at the Prix de Diane, Chantilly, 1991

JACQUES PINTURIER

The Parisian milliner Jacques
Pinturier is far too original to be
described as mainstream. Though at
first glance his creations seem somewhat
bizarre, they work extremely well as
hats because beneath the whimsy is the
skill and knowledge of the trained and
experienced milliner. Pinturier not only
worked with Balenciaga; he also
collaborated with Schiaparelli, the high
priestess of Surrealism, and her
influence is apparent in the hats shown
here. The Japanese hat (left) is as
singular as the uncompromising
rainbow hat (opposite) is elegant.

Opposite Arc en Ciel, 1990

Left Hat design, 1989

Below Hat design, 1990

MANHATTAN STYLE

New York's young designers have brought to millinery a refreshing sense of unselfconscious fun that reflects the zaniness of much of the city's fashion life. Amy Downs is shown below right *wearing one of her entirely non-status creations, surrounded by variations on the theme. She believes that too much 'design' destroys the possibilities of creativity and*

prefers to leave it to the wearer to mould the basic shape to fit her mood or personality.

*Carlos Lewis takes a more formal design approach to produce his highly stylized models (*opposite*). Chic, pacey, elegant, yet tongue-in-cheek, they are the epitome of Manhattan style.*

Opposite Hats by Carlos Lewis, 1991

Below Amy Downs, 1991

The modern millinery world is divided between the haute couture designers, like David Shilling and Philip Treacy, who often produce hats that seem more appropriate to the stage than to even the most fashionable of streets; and more down-to-earth practitioners, such as Amy Downs in New York or Bernstock-Speirs in London. The former are in the same mould as those modern couturiers who create collections of great beauty but of such scant practicality that they often seem to have been made for little more purpose than to be photographed for the glossy magazines. But, like those couturiers, milliners such as Shilling and Treacy are aware that businesses do not survive without a range of hats that can be bought and worn with confidence by ordinary women.

David Shilling is seen by many as millinery's court jester. For many years, his mother enlivened the Ascot season by wearing some of his most extravagant concoctions, which, he claims, he began designing for her at the age of twelve. Huge, and unquestionably eye-catching, they were always humorous and sometimes witty, but it would be wrong to assess Shilling's ability on such extravaganzas. He is a serious professional milliner who has been in business since 1976, and has consistently sold to prestigious stores such as Bloomingdales and Bergdorf Goodman. Although Shilling is frequently ignored by the gurus of the international fashion world, a travelling exhibition of his hats, mounted by the Ulster Museum in 1981, met with considerable success. Shilling's whimsy is not to everyone's taste, and many of his designs seem to make too strong a statement for wearability, but he has always attracted a loyal clientele.

Philip Treacy shares many of Shilling's design characteristics. His hats are highly original and bold, a boldness that can sometimes not be matched by the wearer. Born in Ireland in 1966, Treacy studied fashion at the Royal College of Art in London. During his studies he worked on a millinery project with Harrods, which decided him on his future. His brief career has been spectacular. He designs hats for John Galliano in London and Karl Lagerfeld in Paris and his clientele includes some of the world's richest and most fashionable women.

Sketch by David Shilling.

Treacy was taught by Shirley Hex, the ex-manager of Frederick Fox's studio, as was another up-and-coming young British designer in much the same mould, Nicholas Oakwell. An Australian-born London milliner, Fox has been described by Stephen Jones as 'the milliner with the best technique in the world', and, certainly, he holds an honoured place in London fashion. He is a favourite designer of the British royal family, to whose notice he was brought by the couturier Hardy Amies who has, for many years, designed a high proportion of the Queen's clothes. Fox created the hats for the royal tour of Brazil in 1970, and has been one of the Queen's milliners since that time. Quite apart from the work that this brings him directly – the Queen is probably the only woman who always wears a hat in public – the cachet that comes with being 'By Appointment' to the Queen is considerable. It not only means that London society, wishing to be associated with royalty, patronizes him, but also that women from all over the world follow the trail to his door.

Those who are looking for less formal hats turn to milliners of the calibre of Kirsten Woodward and Viv Knowland, who are both able to express in their designs the mood of the moment. Like Stephen Jones, Woodward is famed for her inventive approach. She spent a valuable creative period in the early 1980s designing hats for Karl Lagerfeld – a time during which she was able to give full rein to her surrealistic imagination. Knowland is less inclined to flamboyance but her relaxed and

Opposite Hat by Stephen Jones, photographed by David Seidner.

Cloche hat in ruby fur felt by Patricia Underwood, 1991.

understated style fits the design approach of many of the London-based couturiers with whom she has worked – most successfully with Betty Jackson's dégagé lines. Probably the most skilful of middle-market milliners is Patricia Underwood. Born in Great Britain, Underwood moved to New York in 1967 and has been based there ever since. Before becoming a hat designer she worked as a secretary at Buckingham Palace – one of the world's last bastions of hatwearing. Underwood's approach is entirely practical. Her paramount concern is how her hats will relate to clothing. 'Why bother to have a hat', she asks, 'if it does not go with the clothes?'

It can be argued that it is the 'little' milliners working out of their own tiny studios and shops who do most to keep millinery alive as part of the street scene. Their hats are handmade and can be specially designed or bought off the peg. Sometimes the uniqueness of a specially designed hat lies in nothing more radical than a particular material or trim. These hatters are true artisans and many, like New York designer Amy Downs, had no formal training in millinery. Consequently, many of their hats are made of soft felt or fabrics that can be easily sewn together as simple berets or cloches. Downs frequently finishes her hats with a knot at the top, which she calls a 'twirly'. She puts her finger on the appeal of this kind of hat when she points out that she wants her hats to be accessible rather than aloof. She claims that people gravitate towards her hats because, with their bright colours and whimsical touches, they are reminiscent of the world of the nursery.

Lola Erlich is another New York milliner with a 'downtown' sensibility. She makes hats that are, by her contention, 'simple and understated but with a sense of humour in the details'. She has, for example, created a hat by turning a bouquet of flowers upside down. An ex-editor of *Vogue Knitting*, Erlich has worked with the unconventional Seventh Avenue designer, Betsey Johnson – whose clothes are renowned for their iconoclastic, offbeat wit. Slightly more 'grown up' is Eric Javits, who made the little red derby for Mia Farrow in *Alice*. His elegant and classic hats are frequently enlivened with a touch of 'glitz' – a cowboy hat covered in silver sequins, for instance. Javits's hats have appeared on the covers of *Vogue*, *W* and *Elle* and sell in high-class stores across the United States to women who are looking for 'statement' headwear.

Just as in the 1980s there was a 'school' of young shoemakers in London, so the early nineties has seen the same phenomenon develop in millinery in New York. A new, young clientele has surfaced and milliners are appearing to service it. Tracey

Tooker's shop on Lexington Avenue caters to many of the customers who came to her first shop in the Hamptons. Caroline Kennedy, Caroline Roehm, Kitty Carlisle Hart and even Imelda Marcos have regularly bought from her, attracted by her formula of classic shapes with unique trims. Victoria DiNardo, one of New York's most successful milliners, also started her business in the early 1980s. Her hats are unashamedly romantic, as is her shop in SoHo, crammed with hats, antique hatboxes and old hat forms that reflect the spirit of the woman who created the bridal headpiece worn by Paulina Porizkova in the advertisements for Estee Lauder perfume. Much more 'funky' is Carlos Lewis, who produces 'one-off' custom-made hats for a discerning and very fashion-conscious clientele.

But New York does not have the monopoly of millinery talent. Tokyo, Paris and London also have their share of creative designers. Of the three, it is undoubtedly Tokyo that encourages the most radical and forward-looking approach to millinery – as is entirely to be expected from a culture that, at the beginning of the 1980s, brought fundamentally new thinking to Western fashion when the second wave of young designers from Japan first showed in Paris. The shock of the new approaches to dress, so dramatically highlighted in the early shows of Comme des Garçons and Yohji Yamamoto, had an immediate effect on designers across the world – not least those working in Paris.

The Japanese approach was a basic reappraisal of every item of clothing and a reassessment of its place in the modern world. They avoided completely the besetting sin of many Western designers, which is to play sterile games on the theme of historicism. Instead, they created new cuts and original lines never before seen in the West. They were equally radical with the design of hats, encouraging milliners to experiment with new materials, shapes and scale in order to produce truly contemporary millinery.

Most successful in the search for hats with no historic precedent was Issey Miyake, the leader of the first Japanese incursion to Paris, who had shown in the French capital since the 1970s. He was the founder of the Japonism movement in fashion and his radical approach to dress was the inspiration for those of his fellow-countrymen who followed him to Paris. Working with the Amsterdam-based designer Maria Blaisse, Miyake produced what were probably the most innovative hats of the eighties.

Blaisse studied textile design in the sixties and, in 1982, began to work with laminates, rubber and synthetic foams. She moved into this area by accident: she became interested in the clothing possibilities of materials not previously associated with dress when she made some firemen's helmets for her children by cutting them out from the inner tube of a tyre. She began to experiment with rubber as a design material and eventually produced a prototype for what became her Flexicap design. It was a rhombus of black rubber, slit across. She took her idea to the tyre manufacturer Vredestein and the company sponsored her research for the next two years. Miyake commissioned her to design the hats for his Spring/Summer collection for 1988 and they created several styles based on the Flexicap. In their timelessness and modernity these made the work of many established milliners look derivative and sterile.

But the milliner who has been most influential in Japan is Akio Hirata. He designs the hats for the collections of most of the second-wave Japanese designers, including Yohji Yamamoto, Comme des Garçons, and Junko Koshino, as well as for Hanae

Mori, who has shown in Paris for two decades. Hirata studied with the French milliner Jean Barthet in the early sixties before founding his own company, Haute Mode Hirata, in 1965. Hirata's hats are all made by hand in his boutique Salon Coco in Hiroo. His approach to design is eclectic and he works with designers either by creating to a specific drawing they have produced or by designing a range of hats to interpret a mood that they have described to him. He also produces his own collection of hats to sell directly to the public. Although not well known in the West, Hirata has an honoured name in Japanese fashion.

Like every other area of fashion today, millinery is an international trade no matter how specific to one culture or country it may at first appear. In London, Carolyn Brookes-Davies and Anita Evagora, whose label is Fred Bare, have a reputation that stretches beyond their tiny shop in the East End. Dustin Hoffman has bought from them and Kylie Minogue appears in one of their creations on the cover of her album, *Enjoy Yourself*. The pair met at the Royal College of Art in 1982. Neither was in the fashion school: Brookes-Davies was studying sculpture and Evagora ceramics. They took up hatmaking initially to finance their art but soon developed into full-time milliners with an annual production of more than 10,000 pieces. The success of their classic bestsellers – a floppy-brimmed suede and a soft Flemish hat – can be judged by the fact that they have been copied at all price ranges in most European countries.

Paris has its own crop of milliners. Like their American and British counterparts, they work to the highest levels of originality but with the advantage of equally high levels of taste and craftsmanship. Jean-Charles Brosseau creates hats that are – like his faux-marble, heavily mirrored shop in the rue de l'Université – elegant as well as trend-setting; Marie Mercié is well established as an international milliner selling in Barney's and Neiman Marcus in the United States; and Gabrielle Cadet, whose business in the place République is visited by all who are seriously interested in fashion, has been described by the U.S. publication, *Women's Wear Daily*, as the city's 'hottest new hatter'. Cadet is one of many milliners making their mark in fashion's capital city. Anna Kaszer sells her light-as-air creations from her shop in the Marais; a short walk away, in the rue des Rosiers, is the boutique of Olivier Chanan, considered by many to be the Parisian milliner of the future. His elegant and mature creations are in the highest traditions of classic French millinery.

Chanan stands comparison with established figures like Jean Barthet and Jacques Pinturier, who share the distinction of being the only milliner members of the Chambre Syndicale de la Couture Parisienne. Barthet is arguably the most successful milliner in Paris. He has had his own establishment for more than forty years and has designed for most of the great couture houses, including Lanvin, Lagerfeld and Ungaro. His dramatic hats appeal to actors, socialites and entertainers, and his customers include Sophia Loren, Catherine Deneuve, Princess Stephanie of Monaco and Michael Jackson. Barthet combines the standards of the past with the esprit of the present. Though his hats never look old-fashioned, they do not achieve modernity at the expense of grace. Pinturier – who worked with Schiaparelli and Balenciaga – takes a different view. 'Today', he declares, 'there are no new hats.' Grand, elitist and eccentric, Pinturier has a mission to uphold the highest standards of millinery and, as he puts it, 'to give back style to hats that Monsieur Dior destroyed by making them accessible'. He might well be thinking of the creations of the legendary Paulette, whose one-time assistant, Josette Desnus, is still making hats

Marie Mercié's trade card.

Hat by Jean Barthet, 1981.

Hat by Tête-à-Tête, 1991.

in her shop Tête-à-Tête in the rue du Faubourg Saint-Honoré. Her clients include most of the those members of the fashionable European aristocracy who patronized Paulette before her death, as well as actors such as Jane Seymour.

Vital as the design input from such milliners is, it is nevertheless the couturiers who keep ahead of – and actually create – the mood of fashion. Supreme among these in terms of millinery is Karl Lagerfeld, who designs for Chanel in Paris and Fendi in Rome, as well as creating his own line. One of fashion's polymaths, Lagerfeld is endlessly creative and original. His exuberant fantasies often flout the rules of good taste, but nothing he designs is ever dull. His millinery has frequently flirted with surrealism and in 1985, working with Kirsten Woodward, he designed a hat in the shape of an armchair to match a dress upholstered like an ottoman. The year before he had produced an amusing series of hats based on traditional French patisserie which echoed Stephen Jones's 'French Fries' hat of the previous year. Their outrageous ideas – truly 'madcap' – are not unique. John Galliano has made hats from materials as unusual as twigs and *objets trouvés*, and has created headpieces that interweave bizarre materials with the model's own hair. Such creations are the stuff of fantasy and are the prerogative of designers who are not trammelled by the need to produce hats that can actually be worn off the catwalk. In Paris, Jean-Paul Gaultier and Christian Lacroix have always given full rein to their imagination. Lacroix is a satirist who makes fun of the traditional elements of glamour: his broad-brimmed picture hat has a brim wider than the model's shoulders and a crown twice the normal height. He piles fruit and flowers impossibly high in a pastiche of the

Sketches by Christian Lacroix.

1940s hats of movie star Carmen Miranda. Although purists may object, it must be remembered that such flights of fantasy are meant to be little more than fun. Though they sometimes encapsulate the fashion mood of the moment, they are never intended to be worn anywhere but in a fashion show.

But the couturiers' world is one of spartra and tulle while the world of the ordinary milliner is one of velvet and felt. Deep-crowned versions of the Annie Hall hat have been recycled a thousand times by small-scale designers eking out a living in Greenwich Village or Covent Garden, designers who often cannot afford a shop and are forced to sell their goods from market stalls. Their customers, also young and impoverished, are searching for a streetwise style, somewhat outlandish but out of the current fashion mould. Although both sexes are happy to wear brilliantly coloured hats embroidered and patterned in Indian style, they do so not solely to add a decorative touch to their clothing. More often they are establishing membership of a group and showing a disaffection with the attitudes of mainstream society. These hats rarely have anything to do with making a fashion statement. Their function is much more to proclaim political and social attitudes. What is more, they are as instantly readable as to the class and social aspirations of the wearers as were their nineteenth-century equivalents.

The twentieth century has been one of protest, in which young people have played an important part. In the 1970s, hippies and 'flower children' used their hats to symbolize their alienation from the mainstream of commercialized urban life. The hippy male wore romantic felt hats based on the nineteenth-century Kossuth. Bohemian and anti-status, such hats made a strong statement simply because of their association with the past. They carried memories of rural homesteaders, Puritan nonconformity and a sense of individuality that seemed in danger of being permanently eclipsed by the exigencies of modern life. Young hippy women chose hats with even more romantic associations – large-brimmed straws, inspired by nineteenth-century Dolly Vardens, which suggested a back-to-nature, antimaterialistic stance. The hats, like the movement itself, were little more than atavistic flights of fancy.

A Hippy, wearing the soft hat that was popular with both sexes.

The Hippies were essentially a middle-class movement. Their protest lacked strength because, instead of reacting to modern urban stresses and attempting to counter them, Hippies frequently seemed to withdraw into a drug-induced dreamworld. Other young people were more rigorous in their response to the difficulties of city life. Antisocial and confrontational, Hell's Angels, skinheads and

Punks fought back. Hell's Angels dressed with all the menace of Nazi stormtroopers, in leather jackets and authoritarian peaked caps. Skinheads chose the traditional knitted woollen cap of the proletariat. In Britain and Germany, skinheads also took the lower-middle-class pork-pie hat and made it part of the menacing uniform of urban violence in much the same way as the bowler became a threatening object in the film *Clockwork Orange*. So sinister was the skinhead aura that the pork-pie hat – which they favoured with a narrow curled brim and worn a size too small – was transformed from a comical item of headwear into something disturbing, with implications that far transcended the suburban limitations of its original wearers.

But the most distinctive of all modern 'street' hats is surely the enormous beret or peaked cap of the Rastafarian, known as a crown. Originating in Jamaica, the Rastafarian movement was named after Ras Tafari who, in 1930, was crowned Haile Selassie, Emperor of Ethiopia. To whites, both the elaborately teased hair ('dreadlocks') and the 'teacosy' hat into which it is crammed originally seemed little more than a black cult fashion. In fact, Rastafarianism is a religious and cultural movement and the Rastafarian hat is not an article of fashion at all but a religious garment, like the Jew's skullcap. As such, its basic shape remains fixed. The only real variations possible are in materials – usually leather or knitted wool. Strict Rastafarians do not allow variations in colour. Knitted caps are always in red, yellow and green – the colours of the Ethiopian banner.

The Rastafarian hat is meant as a clear manifestation of black awareness, a symbol that reminds black people of their origins. Paradoxically, this 'return to the roots' spirit has almost as strong a hold on white youth, who show their sympathy for the culture and philosophy of minorities and the countries of the Third World by wearing hats inspired by ethnic styles. Beanies, skullcaps and pillboxes have all been used to express this solidarity, but it is the peaked baseball cap that has absorbed all trends. It is a classic shape for the young and comes beaded, sequined and embroidered in as many ways as there are minorities. The baseball cap has its own integrity and has even survived the indignity of being shown by Karl Lagerfeld as an accompaniment to his variations on the classic Chanel suit.

The baseball hat perfectly reflects the fall and rise of the hat in the second half of the twentieth century. Although hats from milliners and couturiers are frequently stylish and dramatic, they are often seen as irrelevant. They may, like works of art, be looked at and admired, but they have little other function. Nevertheless, the desire to wear a hat for show is clearly as strong as the need to make a statement about one's attitudes. Hats have not been entirely consigned to history's trashcan, even if millinery effectively has. The fact that more young people than ever now wear them tells its own tale. The baseball hat and its variations might well hold hope for the future. Will the young who wear it today turn to milliners for a substitute as they grow older? If they do, it is to be hoped that there will still be some hatmakers around to answer the call.

The Borsalino baseball cap, with 'Borsalino Wacky' logo, 1990s.

Following pages

Philip Treacy feather hat worn at Ascot, 1991 (*left*), and the original model (*opposite*).

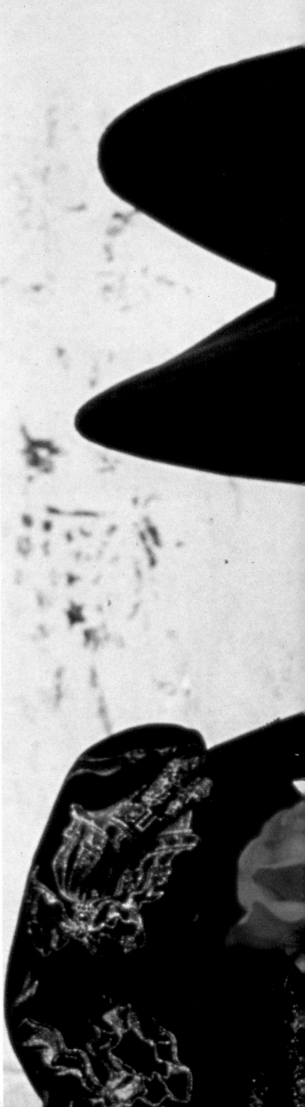

PARISIAN STYLE

*Jean Barthet (*above*) is a highly respected Parisian milliner. His work has long been an example for other designers and his influence can be seen in the work of many new young hatters. Although some of Barthet's most memorable hats have an extravagance that may at first suggest that he is a fantasist above all else, this is far from being the case. Barthet creates in the classic manner of French hatmakers, whereby the severity of line essential to all good millinery is tempered by highly imaginative — and even capricious — trims. In Barthet's showroom, it is easy to be convinced that life is one long race meeting or wedding — or to feel that it should be, so that women have as many opportunities as possible to wear such delicious concoctions.*

*Marie Mercié (*right*) shares much of Barthet's wit. She also has created many memorable hats, some of which, like the hat shown here, play games with scale. Her tongue-in-cheek approach to design ensures Mercié a ready following and she has an international list of fashionable young customers who respond to her iconoclastic approach.*

Above Jean Barthet creating a hat for Sophia Loren, 1991

Opposite Marie Mercié, wearing one of her own hats

HAIR AS HAT

Hair has frequently been treated as a hat. In the 18th century, when hairstyles reached unprecedented proportions, they were so elaborate that the hat became almost redundant. In the 20th century, hair has been teased and moulded into extraordinary shapes by people as far apart as Rastafarians and French haute-couture designers. David Hinds, of the British reggae band Steel Pulse, shaped his own hair with spectacular results but, as Hinds points out, the effect is to do with culture and religion rather than with fashion. Yves Saint Laurent used similarly shaped hair in his 1967 collection for effects that show fashion at its most extreme and unrealistic.

Opposite Rastafarian hairstyle, 1980s

This page Yves Saint Laurent models, 1967

Clockwise, *from top left*
'Cagliostra', 'Turban Cocteau',
'Calot', 'Mildred', 'Untitled',
'Bobine', 'Bibi Parisien',
'Abucodonosor', 'Noemie',
'Ni vus ni pris'

OLIVIER CHANAN

*The traditional characteristics of a good hat are wit and
style. They are hard to achieve: wit is so easily reduced to
vulgarity and style frequently ends up as meaningless
extravagance. The home of all true millinery skills is still
thought by many to be Paris, just as it has been for so long.
The view is debatable — many excellent milliners now work in
New York and London — but these hats by Olivier Chanan
suggest that there may be some truth in the contention.*

*What gives Chanan's hats their indefinable but
immediately recognized spirit is control. No element is
allowed to overrun the others in the overall design. Shape,
trim and line are all given equal consideration in order to
produce millinery that is deceptively simple in appearance.
The apparent ease of Chanan's designs may persuade the
onlooker that not much skill is involved but, in fact, it is this
very simplicity that speaks of the expert.*

GRAHAM SMITH

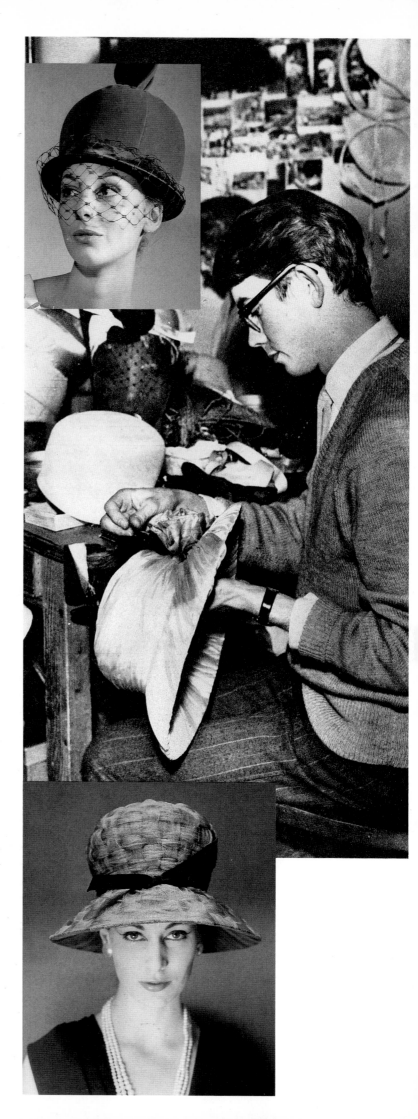

The London milliner Graham Smith works to the highest standards of Paris couture but tempers them with the softness of traditional English dress. Although his hats have chic, they are never hard or cold. Smith's fashion sense is second to none, but he does not set out to make a fashion statement at the expense of the wearer. He believes that if a hat does not become part of a woman, it has failed, no matter how well it might photograph for the fashion magazines.

Smith's hats are about line, not decorative fantasy, which is why, in a showroom, they can sometimes look low-keyed. It is only when they are being worn that their true flattery is revealed in the way in which their lines encompass the head and join the back curve of the neck — a crucial point in millinery, often ignored by milliner and customer alike. It is a measure of their sophistication that the essence of Graham Smith's hats could be captured by an artist with one uninterrupted brush stroke, as simple and effective as a Hokusai wave. It is no surprise to learn that the greatest influence on Smith was Balenciaga, the fashion purist of the 20th century, though he admits to learning the basic rules of fashion during this 7-year association with the couturier Michael of Carlos Place. Michael was Smith's mentor and it is from him that he has inherited his sense of style, best summed up in the Diana Vreeland phrase 'the necessity for refusal' — an elegance of mind that makes a designer pare down rather than pile on.

This page Graham Smith in Paris at Lanvin-Castillo, 1960s

Inset top Hat design for Michael, Winter 1960

Right Hat design, 1958

Opposite page Designs for Kangol, 1980s–1992

SURREALIST SHELLS

The shape of a shell is so satisfyingly complete that it is not surprising that it has so often provided inspiration for hat designers. It moulds the head and flatters the face; it brings with it echoes of Botticelli's Primavera; *it is essentially romantic and feminine.*

This form has attracted some of the world's greatest couturiers, including Dior and Balenciaga. The examples shown here are all from designers known for their fantasy: Mariucca Mandelli of Krizia, Karl Lagerfeld at Chanel and Christian Lacroix. It is clearly the element of surrealism, as well as the decorative satisfaction to be gained from putting a shell on a woman's head, that appeals to designers of their calibre.

Above Krizia, 1980

Opposite main picture Karl Lagerfeld, ready-to-wear, Spring/Summer 1991

Inset Christian Lacroix, couture, Summer 1988

Sybilla, Spring/Summer 1991

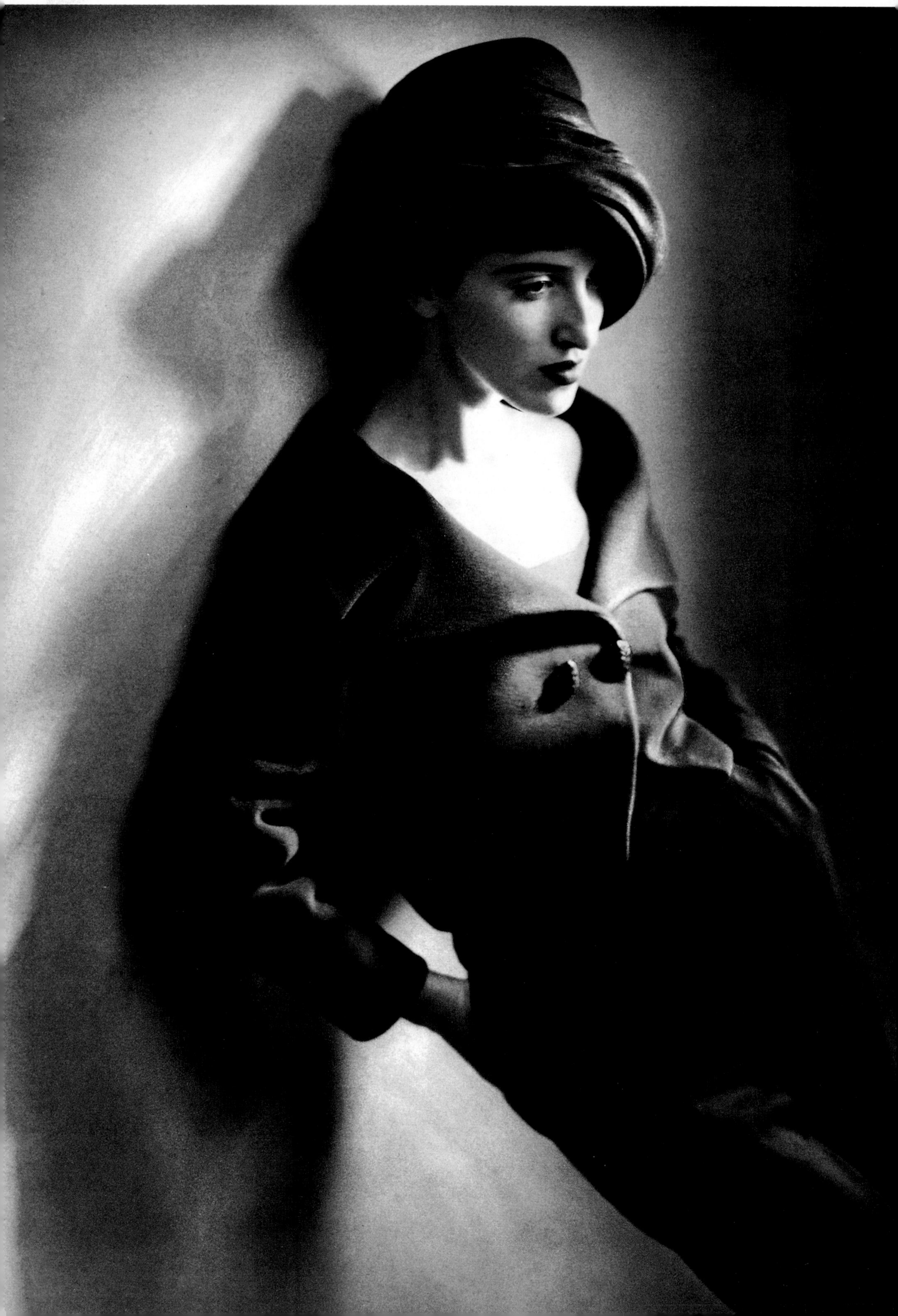

SYBILLA

The Spanish designer Sybilla came to the fore in the mid-1980s as part of the 'unstructured' movement in European fashion, a movement based on the principle that clothes should follow the body's natural contours rather than use padding to create an artificial shape. Its practitioners have always enjoyed juxtaposing simple body draping with extravagance on the head and Sybilla has created many show-stopping hats which, in their scale and purity of line, recall those of her illustrious Spanish predecessor, the couturier Balenciaga.

STREET STYLE

Since the early 1970s it has frequently been claimed that millinery is dead – or, at least, dying. This claim is open to question, but what is not in dispute is the fact that hats are still a thriving part of the urban street scene, kept alive by young hatters and their customers who are found in increasing numbers in all

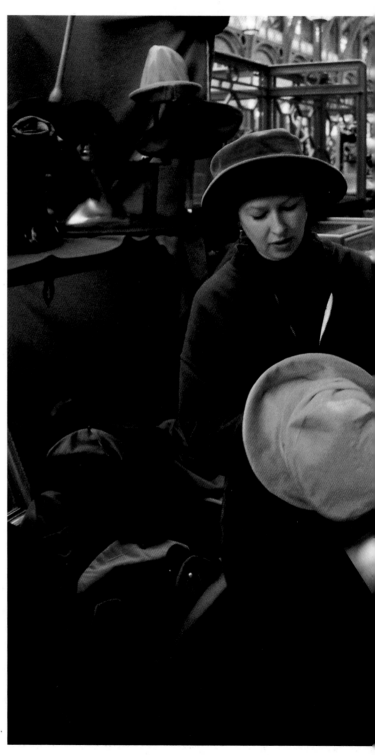

Left Rollerskater, 1980

Above Market stall milliner, 1992

Right above Acid house party, Manchester, 1991

Right below Street styles, 1992

the major cities of the world. The impetus for these new, informal, non-status hats comes from the world of music and sport – two of the bedrocks of youth culture. The most popular styles are soft and flexible, allowing scope for individuality in how the hat is worn; the favourite material is velvet and the top colours are black, purple, wine and brown. Such hats are seen in Greenwich Village, Covent Garden and the Marais on the heads of the liveliest and most confident-looking young people. Those who are not wearing this relaxed style are almost certainly sporting the most talismanic youth hat of all – the baseball cap.

CHRONOLOGY OF THE HAT

before 1100

MEN

Until the 12th century men rarely wear any headwear except the simple Phrygian bonnet – a cap of conical shape with the top turned forward. It is normally made of wool or felt.

WOMEN

Women are always expected to cover their heads and usually do so by draping a broad scarf or veil around head and shoulders so that only the face is visible. These scarves and veils are often brightly coloured. Crowns and coronets are worn over them. By the 11th century, the veil has evolved into the more refined couvre-chef, or kerchief, which has a straight edge hanging over the forehead and can be wound around the face like a scarf. Like its predecessor, it leaves no hair showing.

1100–1200

MEN

The hood emerges as a separate entity. It is a loose, pointed cowl, frequently with a cape attached that covers the shoulders. Although the Phrygian cap is still common wear it is now joined by small round caps not unlike modern berets. For travelling, a large-brimmed hat is often worn over the hood. Towards the end of the century, the coif appears. A small, close-fitting bonnet of linen, it covers the head and ties under the chin. (It survives well into the 15th century on the heads of various learned professionals.)

WOMEN

The veil remains throughout the century, modified by the introduction of the barbette and fillet, which consists of a linen band across the temples and under the chin, worn with a linen circlet around the head. It is the precursor of the wimple. Made of fine material such as linen or silk, the wimple covers neck and bosom and is drawn up around the face and pinned to the hair under a veil. The wimple frequently covers the chin as well as the neck and, because of its all-concealing effect, is often used as mourning wear.

1200–1300

MEN

The hood, small round cap, large-brimmed travelling hat and coif remain with slight variations in style.

WOMEN

Hairstyles become much more elaborate and, though no new styles of headwear emerge, the earlier styles are modified to take account of this. The fillet is adapted to accommodate the new, broader hairstyles and loses its circular shape.

1300–1400

MEN

The style of the hood changes to produce what to modern eyes is the first recognizable male headgear of the Middle Ages: the liripipe, an extension of the point of the hood's cowl which hangs according to its cut. If cut vertically, it falls to the side; if horizontally, it hangs straight. It later grows very long and is then wrapped around the head rather like a turban.

Towards the end of the century the hood is worn in such a way as to make a turban shape with the facial opening and edges rolled up to cover only the top of the head. The fashion statement of this style is made by the gorget which falls in folds over one shoulder and can be made to stand upright, fanned out above the head. Its edge is normally dagged. Plumes begin to appear on the hats of the rich. They are usually ostrich or peacock feathers and are frequently secured by jeweled brooches. In addition to felt, the hats of the very rich are made of the newly imported beaver.

WOMEN

The barbette is increasingly discarded and headwear consists of the fillet and a fret, a hairnet that covers the hair, which is now coiled around the ears. For travel, hoods are worn. These are also standard wear for countrywomen and the poor.

1400–1500

MEN

Most courts in Europe are now in thrall to fashion – especially the styles worn in other countries – and fashionable men spend vast amounts of time and money on clothes. There is an explosion of new fashions but for the most part they are variations on already existing styles. The hood remains but on a gradually reduced scale. The new small hood, buttoned in front, is worn thrown back by the stylish, so as to make a kind of muffler round the neck. Less fashionable men continue to wear the liripipe, often dagged, and in strong colours and rich materials such as velvet and damask.

The chaperon develops from the hood-turban and for at least fifty years is the hat of power as well as fashion. It consists of the burlet – a stuffed and padded circular brim – and the gorget, or gole, which either hangs limp on the opposite side to the liripipe (which still survives) or is stiffened to stand up in the cockscomb manner. A frequent variation is the chaplet, usually dagged and ornamented with jewels. Hats come into their own in this century and the most prestigious is undoubtedly the high-crowned, broad-brimmed beaver, shaped almost like an hourglass. By the end of the century caps, known as bonnets, have become popular with young men who usually favour the Turkey bonnet, based on a fez.

WOMEN

Veils become more elaborate – even architectural – and are frequently shaped into a squared goffered arch that is the precursor of the Tudor arch headpiece. Another style that appears at the end of the century and foreshadows a look common in the next is the chaplet headdress, consisting of a padded roll worn over the fret. The fret itself (frequently referred to as a caul) is a universal fashion by now and can be interlaced in remarkably complicated patterns. An increase in elaborate headdress totally eclipses the hair itself.

Padded, cushion headdress; nets enclosing the hair; horned headdress; circular, sausage-shaped rolls and wired veils are all testimony to the increasing interest in the head as a fashion focal point. In the second half of the century, height becomes the fashion and tall, backward-tilted headwear worn high on the head is seen throughout Europe. The new styles are in imitation of the French hennin, a tall cone like the Victorian dunce's cap. It is followed by chimneypot styles, butterfly headdress and turbans in an effort to obtain the height so essential to the fashionable silhouette. By the end of the century, headdress has become as high as physically possible and the other extreme – the low, hood-like covering – is beginning to replace it.

1500–1550

MEN

The archetypal hat is the low, soft style normally called a bonnet. It usually has a small brim characteristically turned up all round so that the shape is neat and gives the appearance of being head-hugging. There are many variations, of which the most popular is the buttoned cap. This, though far from stylish, is worn across Europe as the general, all-purpose male headgear. For more showy occasions, its place is taken by the Milan bonnet, a soft crowned affair with a broad, turned-up brim, slit at each side to form a clearly distinct front and back portion sometimes joined by aiglets. The brim is trimmed at the front with a brooch or jewelled medallion. It is a style for noblemen and spawns other bonnet styles with slashed brims.

In all countries the male bonnet is a prestigious affair with elaborate trimmings of feathers, lace and ribbons. By mid-century a more sophisticated style has been introduced from Italy: the flat cap, a simple but perfect shape worn tilted to one side and trimmed only in most restrained fashion.

WOMEN

The century dawns quietly, with headwear low and understated. Most developments are centred on the hood, which is usually made of stiffened linen often shaped to form an arch that frames the face and frequently worn with a barbe, a pleated linen bib that covers the chin. The standard hood shape, known in Europe as the English hood, is strongly architectural, formed like a gable or pediment and often heavily embroidered. In its later forms, this hood becomes very rigid and the space under the gable is covered by material. On no account is any hair shown.

The French hood is smaller and worn further off the brow. It is far less rigid than the English style and follows the contours of the brow. (It is this hood that is always associated with Mary Stuart, though the style she adopted – which was normally followed by Englishwomen – had a straight wired border with a dip in the centre of the forehead and the top of the crown flattened across the head.)

An interesting variation on the French hood is the bongrace – a curtain of material folded flat on the head so that one end forms a straight line across the forehead and the other falls at the back of the head.

1550–1600

MEN

The most characteristic style is the court bonnet which has a high crown and a small, stylishly rolled brim. It is normally decorated with precious stones or jewels and frequently has the extra trim of a small plume worn at the front or side. It is the forerunner of the most fashionable hat of the sixteenth century: the copotain, or sugar loaf. It is made of felt, has a high crown and a brim. Beaver hats, with large crowns and wide brims, continue as status hats largely because of their cost but are not usually worn by the fashionable young. The flat cap, known in London as the 'City flat cap', continues to be worn and becomes standard headwear.

WOMEN

The lettice cap (named after the fur from which it was made, a form of ermine) becomes fashionable. It is a bonnet-shaped article with a triangular crown that curves forward over the ears. Other popular styles are the caul, which fits closely to the head and is decorated with gold thread, pearls and jewels; the coif, and the crespin, a caul worked in gold and usually embroidered. Towards the end of the century women begin to wear hats based on men's styles. The tall, high-crowned hats of courtiers are copied for women, with jewelled hatbands and ostrich feather trim.

1600–1650

MEN

Hats reach new heights of extravagance. The scale is voluminous and the trim costly. The large hat with a high crown and broad brim, later to be known as the 'Cavalier', is the dominant style. In the middle of the century its popularity is rivalled by the copotain, now known as the sugar loaf. Hats are made of various materials, including the expensive beaver. More mundane materials such as felt and shag (made of worsted or, occasionally, of silk or hair) and, more richly, velvet and silk are also used. Luxurious trims are common, particularly using feathers. The favourites are ostrich feathers, worn either singly or in bunches that drape around the brim or stand upright and droop over the crown. The other prestigious and expensive trim is the hatband, which can be of anything from silk and crewel cords or ribbons to buttons and gold or silver wire.

WOMEN

At the beginning of the century, the Mary Stuart and the French hood are both still popular. A softer and less formal style is the kerchief, a large, lace-trimmed handkerchief placed on the head so that the edges fall free at either side. A variation of this fashion is the plain gauze veil informally draped over the head and face. Hoods, known as chaperones, are common. Made of soft material tied with a bow under the chin, they are frequently worn over a coif.

The large-brimmed hat, a copy of the 'cavalier' hat, is worn by fashionable women. The male sugar-loaf style is often worn with a coif or undercap to protect it from grease from the hair.

1650–1700

MEN

In the last decade of the century, the cocked hat, known today as the tricorne, makes its appearance. Its shape is triangular; it is cocked symmetrically and usually has a fringe of ostrich along the brim.

WOMEN

In the 1680s, the fontage becomes the most glamorous headcovering.

1700–1750

MEN

The century is dominated by the wig, and hats, though still worn, are not central to fashion. The chief style is the tricorne – deep crowned and with the brim cocked on all three sides. It is called by various names depending on how it is cocked. The brim is bound with lace or braid and occasionally has a jewel or feather ornament. Cocked hats are usually large and showy, but smaller versions also appear. Not all brimmed hats are cocked and many men, according to age and class, continue to wear round hats with either stiff or slouched brims.

Top quality hats are made of beaver but cheaper hats, known as demi-castors (a mixture of beaver and coney) are common. Most men's hats are trimmed or edged with braid or metal lace of varying quality and cost.

As men normally have their heads shaved in order to wear a wig, night caps (sometimes referred to as morning caps) are worn at home when the wig has been removed. Made of linen, cotton, silk or velvet, they are not unlike turbans and have high crowns. They are not worn in bed.

WOMEN

Indoors, caps are worn. For outdoor wear the same caps are worn under hats. These caps, known as day caps, are normally made of linen and almost invariably edged with lace. They often have lappets – two streamers either hanging behind or pinned to the crown of the cap – and a border of coloured ribbon. They are sometimes ornamented with artificial flowers. The coif – a rudimentary bonnet that hugs the contours of the head – is common, worn especially by countrywomen. The most characteristic headwear is the mob cap, a large-crowned headcovering with a deep border and with ties known as kissing strings.

Outdoor hats are normally worn over a day cap and tend to be small. Straw and silk examples, with shallow crowns and tiny brims, are found through the century but there is also a vogue for the self-consciously rustic straw hat called the bergere, which originated in France. It has a flat crown and a wide brim and is usually tied under the chin by ribbons. Despite its antecedents, it is a sophisticated hat, worn in town as much as in the country.

1750–1800

MEN

In the 1770s, the tricorne begins to go out of fashion, forced aside by the Nivernois, the bicorne – frequently referred to as the chapeau bras – and the tall round hat that has evolved for riding but is increasingly worn as a fashionable hat for town. The tall hat is always flat-topped with an uncocked brim. The best models are made of beaver and have only a hatband and an occasional cockade as decoration. This is the first hint of the top hat to come.

WOMEN

In the last decades of the century, the dormeuse, a mob cap from France, becomes all the rage. It is very large and elaborately trimmed with layers of lace and ruching. Like all caps at this time, it consists of a crown or 'bag', a frill or 'wing', and lappets. Though the dormeuse is large, wigs are frequently larger, and it is often perched on the top of a vast edifice of artificial hair. In strong contrast, the butterfly cap is very small. Made of lace, it is wired into a butterfly shape and worn perched well forward on the forehead.

As wigs grow bigger, many fashionable women abandon hats altogether. Those who do not have to wear them tilted at an extreme angle and often elaborately beribboned and trimmed with flowers – a style that has become known as the Gainsborough hat. They are usually enormous, as their names – the ballon, the parachute or the Lunardi (after the French balloonist) – suggest; they are made of straw, beaver and felt and are trimmed with ribbons, bows and feathers.

1800–1850

MEN

The top hat dominates the 19th century as thoroughly as the tricorne dominated the 18th. However, it is by no means a static style and variations in scale both of brim and crown are found throughout the century.

In the 1820s, the Wellington is popular. A high hat, it slopes inwards towards the top and has a narrow curled brim. A variant, known as the Turf, is distinguished by its wider brim, which curves sharply up. The Cumberland or 'pointed hat' has a crown 8 inches high and a very narrow turned-up brim. At the beginning of the century, hats with smaller, flat-topped crowns and broad brims are in vogue. The chapeau bras has survived as the opera hat – not to be confused with the top hat with a collapsible crown that appears in 1848. Also in the 1840s, the low-crowned, wide-brimmed wide-awake becomes popular. By mid-century, deerstalkers and Glengarries are popular country and sporting wear. In 1850 the first bowler is made by Lock & Co., London.

WOMEN

The mob cap continues its reign. Variations on the basic shape are the Biggin, which has no lappets and is not tied, and the Cornette, shaped like a bonnet and tied under the chin. Toques and turbans are popular. Often, women wear only a handkerchief pinned to the head and ornamented with flowers for evening occasions.

The bonnet dominates the first decades of the century; the most popular style being the Capote, which has a large soft crown and a stiff brim. The most commonly seen type of bonnet has a high, stiff crown and deep brim and is universally known as the poke bonnet. In the 1820s, fashionable hats and bonnets suddenly become huge and are smothered in ribbons, flowers, feathers and gauze trims to give an even greater sense of bulk. Bonnets frequently have the addition of a bavolet, a fall of soft material attached to the back of the crown and covering the back of the neck.

1850–1900

MEN

By the beginning of the 1870s, top hats have become much smaller and are frequently called 'chimney pots'. A unique top hat style is the one with a truncated crown – cut to half its size – known in England as a Muller Cut-Down, after a famous murderer called Muller who was apprehended as a result of wearing this unusual style. As the century draws to its close, the topper, wide-awake (sometimes known in the United States as a Jim Crow) and bowler lose ground to the homburg, a stiff felt with a dent running from front to back of the crown, much favoured by the Prince of Wales, and the trilby, a soft felt with an indented low crown named after the hat worn by Beerbohm Tree in the play of that name by George du Maurier. Another low-crowned hat taking its name from a play is the fedora, with its central crease from front to back of the crown, inspired by Sardou's play *Fedora*, first performed in 1881. Straw hats – including the boater – are popular summer wear.

WOMEN

By mid-century, the scale has reduced and the hat has lost ground to the bonnet which is now very deep-brimmed. Veils in black or white, worn down to cover the face or thrown back from the brim, are a strong fashion. Caps continue to be worn indoors; they are frequently embroidered or trimmed with lace and ribbons. By the 1860s, hats have gone out of style and modishly dressed women wear only bonnets. The bavolet is now a standard part of the design. An unusual development is the 'ugly' – a second, detachable brim added to the bonnet to protect the wearer from the sun.

Hats come back into fashion as informal headwear in the early 1870s. Straw sailor hats and wide-brimmed bergeres are popular. Small Tyrolean hats in velvet and silk, with tiny, pertly turned-up brims, are considered rather 'fast' and most women prefer the more staid Glengarry or pork-pie.

It is in the 1870s that the explosion of women's hat styles takes place. By far the best known today is the Dolly Varden, worn with a very wide brim and a flat crown, but variations on the basic bonnet styles are legion. The Charlotte Corday in velvet or the Capote, with its soft crown, are both very popular – as is the toque. As the century closes, the homburg and flower pot become extremely fashionable styles. Hats are increasingly trimmed with feathers and most fashionable hats require a veil.

1900–1914

MEN

The top hat, bowler, homburg, fedora and trilby cross into the new century. No new fashion appears before World War I except the panama.

WOMEN

The art of millinery is pushed to its outermost limits in the first decade of the new century, though things begin quietly enough. At the start of the century the fashionable hat in Paris, London and New York is the small hat that perches on the head and is at its most chic in black, with a small veil. By 1910, most hats are enormous, though Poiret's tight turban ornamented with an aigrette, seen on the most fashionable heads in Paris, is an exception.

Scale is still important at all social levels and is provided by trims. Feathers, artificial flowers, waxed satin ribbons and tulle are all used in abundance on hats as well as toques, the latter newly fashionable again and worn large and tilted back off the face. By 1914, the number and variety of hat styles rivals those of the late 19th century.

1915–1930

MEN

After World War I, the top hat is worn for only the most formal occasions, its place having been taken by the bowler. The boater goes into eclipse, overshadowed by the panama, and the trilby takes the lead as the 'all purpose', classless hat of the new man of the century in Europe and North America. The 20th-century trilby is made less formal than the late 19th-century version by a narrower brim.

WOMEN

In the 1920s the cloche becomes the most fashionable hat for both younger and older women. For summer recreational occasions a broader-brimmed picture hat is often worn.

1930–1939

MEN

By the mid-1930s, the trilby, often known as the snap-brim, is almost the universal hat for town and business wear. In the country, tweed sports caps and traditional cloth caps are the norm.

WOMEN

The cloche is abandoned in the early years in favour of wide brims and more decorative variations. By the middle of the decade the general tendency is for hats to be high and modestly scaled, taking as their model the hats of the Tyrol, the fez and the sailors' hat. Berets, pillboxes and tricornes are fashionable – the latter marking a move towards the asymmetric lines that are to be a theme of the decade. Towards the end of the period crowns become tall and often pointed and brims are reduced. The fashionable hat is a slouch, worn with the brim pulled down over one eye. Turbans of jersey and hoods and snoods (often of over-scale crochet) are all popular at the outset of World War II and are destined to remain the basic styles for the next five years.

1939–1945

WOMEN

With the fall of Paris in 1940, the flow from the fountainhead of fashion is temporarily cut off and millinery re-runs the styles of the 1930s. But the period is remarkable for the ingenuity shown by the Parisians during the German occupation. As an act of defiance, to show that French fashion cannot be killed, they take the turban as their rallying point and wear it draped as high as possible.

Many of the 1940s turbans are ad hoc affairs using any materials to hand, including paper flowers, cellophane and offcuts of pre-war materials.

More down-to-earth turbans become the protective headwear of women factory workers in Britain and North America. Military headwear also has an influence and many peaked-cap styles for women are remarkably similar to those worn by men on active service.

1945–1960

MEN

After the war, men wear hats only rarely and, by the beginning of the 1950s, the fashion for hat wearing almost entirely disappears. Although certain age groups and classes continue to wear them – and though there are occasional and local crazes, such as the revival of the bowler in London – the fashion never regains its former position.

WOMEN

For women, the 1950s brings the introduction of the urchin cut, which signals the beginning of the reign of hair that will finally destroy the necessity for, or even the desirability of, a hat. But the hat dies slowly. Hat styles of the 1950s complement the long slim lines of the clothes styles of the time by being either very small – flat pancake berets and pillboxes – or very large – romantic picture hats in the spirit of the turn of the century. The coolie hat, introduced by Balenciaga, is an important fashion influence, universally copied at high street level in cheap stiff straw.

1960–1970

MEN AND WOMEN

The prevailing tendency is towards unisex clothing. The 'Beatles' cap – named after the pop group – an ordinary peaked cap based on the army officer's service cap, is worn by young people of both sexes. More formal women's styles are the pillbox, worn especially in the U.S., where it is popularized by Jackie Kennedy, and huge 'Doctor Zhivago' hats of wolf, fox and imitation fur – basically overscale toques – which are the 'glamour' statement of the decade. Cowboy and homesteader hats with broad brims are popular casual wear, as are handkerchiefs and scarves pulled tightly across the brow, pirate-fashion. Soft, pull-on hats such as those sold in the London boutique Biba are popular in the last few years of the decade as part of the 'romantic' look. They are frequently seen in knitted, anti-fashion form.

1970–1980

MEN AND WOMEN

Patchwork appears on hats and berets to join sequins and embroidery as part of the burgeoning ethnic movement. The strongest look is the felt hat, often appliqued with pop music symbols. Soft, tweed, pull-on styles based on the 'Annie Hall' look are popular at the end of the decade. The male fedora is plagiarized by milliners in a variety of fabrics, from felt to straw, often with paisley printed scarves tied around the crown. 'Retro' looks become fashionable, including the 1920s cloche and the 1930s slouch hat. Knitted, crocheted and felt hats are popular.

1980–1990

MEN AND WOMEN

A revival of more formal hatwearing in Great Britain occurs under the influence of the Princess of Wales. Her small, brimmed felt hat, usually decorated with a feather, is widely copied. The baseball cap is the most popular style for the young of both sexes. Fedoras continue to be worn, as do broad-brimmed felts and sombreros. Small, informal hatters popularize variations on the soft Rembrandt beret in velvet, felt and suede.

ACKNOWLEDGMENTS

Books are not written in a vacuum and this one is no exception. In order to write it I have read widely in diaries and memoirs as well as consulting some of the many thousands of costume books written in the last 200 years.

I am grateful for the opportunity to consult magazines, periodicals and scarce books in the Victoria and Albert Museum and the British Library. As always, even the most arcane queries have been dealt with quickly and efficiently by the London Library. But I must single out for special thanks the librarian and staff at New York's Fashion Institute of Technology for their unfailing courtesy and help in guiding me through their unequalled resources.

No one researching a book on the English hat industry in general and straw hats in particular can do so without visiting the library of the Luton Museum and I am grateful to Stephen Bunker, the archivist, and Marion Nicholls, the Keeper of Social History, for their interest and help as well as for allowing me to visit them for long periods at a time.

It is essential to talk to milliners, hatters and those in the trade who know the little pieces of 'inside' information that rarely get into books. In this I was lucky enough to speak with key figures on both sides of the Atlantic. In England, John Christie-Miller gave most generously of his time, telling me a great deal about the 'trade' end of the hat business; he also lent me some extremely useful books. In New York, I must single out Benjamin Fay, Janine Gallimard, Harold Koda, Beatrice Lasson, Kai Loften, Marjorie Miller and Woody Shelp for their kindness. It was a great privilege also to talk to John P. John, who reminisced freely about his days as a milliner and gave me much 'period' detail.

Helen Adie did invaluable research in Paris and Pat Murgatroyd found me some apt and unusual quotations. The manuscript was typed at great speed and with cheerful efficiency by Carrie Jimminson. To her and all the other people who helped I extend a warm thanks.

The publishers would like to thank the following for their help in the preparation of this book, and in particular the designers and companies who generously made available original sketches and photographs from their archives:
Jean Barthet, Bates Hatters, Boon & Lane, Ian Bromley, Olivier Chanan, Dr Yolande Crowe, Amy Downs, Frederick Fox, Herbert Johnson Ltd, Hermès, Madame M. T. Hirschkoff, Paris; Stephen Jones, Charlotte Knight, Nick Knight, Christian Lacroix, Lanvin, Oscar Lewis, Lock & Co., Madame E. Lorant, Paris, Yuki Maekawa at Comme des Garçons, Marie Mercié, Philippe Model, Jacques Pinturier, Yvette Powell at the Rasta Society, London; David Seidner, David Shilling, Graham Smith, Damian Stephens, Sybilla, Philip Treacy, Patricia Underwood.

PHOTOGRAPHIC ACKNOWLEDGMENTS

By courtesy of Balenciaga, Paris, p. 132; By courtesy of Jean Barthet, Paris, pp. 202, 196; By courtesy of Bates Hatters, London, pp. 62, 142; By courtesy of Boon and Lane, Luton, England, pp. 59, 63; Berlin, Museum für Völkerkunde, pp. 44, 111; By courtesy of Borsalino, pp. 56, 199; Boston, Museum of Fine Arts, p. 27; Henry Bourne, p. 107; Bulloz, pp. 13, 51, 146; Camera Press, p. 85; By courtesy of Carlos, New York Hats, pp. 69, 190; By courtesy of Olivier Chanan, Paris, pp. 206–7, p. 206 model Sasja (Diva), photo Sarah Wells, Paris; J. L. Charmet, Paris, pp. 15, 74, 81, 99, 101, 114, 122, 151,160, 164; By courtesy of Comme des Garçons, p. 184, photo Minsei Tominaga, from *Six*, issue 2, 1988; Copenhagen, National Museum pp. 65, 111, 130; Paul Antoine Decraene/Hermès, pp. 186–7; Deutsche Presse-Agentur/Camera Press, pp. 85, 86; By courtesy of Christian Dior, Paris, p. 152; By courtesy of Amy Downs, New York, p. 191; Frederic Dumas/Hermès, Paris, pp. 106, 118–119, 188–189; Mary Evans Picture Library, pp. 28, 60; Florence, Uffizi, pp. 60–61; By courtesy of Frederick Fox, p. 64; Peter Fraenkel, p. 44; Chantal Fribourg, Paris, pp. 155, 166, 167, 172; By courtesy of John Galliano, p. 133; By courtesy of Jean-Paul Gaultier, p. 137; Giraudon, pp. 37, 146 ; By courtesy of Givenchy, Paris, pp. 61, 83; Greenwich, National Maritime Museum, p. 10; *The Guardian*, p. 90; Hamburg, Kunsthalle, p. 95; Hannover, Niedersächsische Landesgalerie, p. 136; By courtesy of Hermès, Paris, p. 118–119; Horst P. Horst, New York, p. 171; Hulton-Deutsch Picture Library, pp. 58, 59, 91, 198; By courtesy of Mr John, New York, p. 159; By courtesy of Stephen Jones, London, p. 183, photo Nick Knight; Nick Knight, p. 176; Peter Korniss, Budapest, pp. 109, 130; Andy Kyle/Camera Press, p. 181; By courtesy of Christian Lacroix, Paris, pp. 18, 41, 68, 197, 211; By courtesy of Karl Lagerfeld, Paris, 179, 211; By courtesy of Lanvin, Paris, pp. 68, 168–169; Charles Lénars, Paris, pp. 18, 19, 33, 40; By courtesy of James Lock & Co., pp. 55, 67, 95; London, British Museum, pp. 122–3, 132: Imperial War Museum, p. 42: National Gallery, p. 17: National Portrait Gallery, pp. 11, 40: Victoria and Albert Museum, p. 46; Lourdes, Musée des Pyrénées, p. 41; Malmaison, Musée, pp. 12, 136; Mansell Collection, pp. 52, 59, 124; By courtesy of Marie Mercié, Paris, pp. 108–109, photo Claude Genet, p. 203, photo Christine Spengler, 196; R. Michaud/John Hillelson, pp. 110–111; By courtesy of Issey Miyake, p. 133; By courtesy of Philippe Model, pp. 186–187; Christian Moser, p. 107; By courtesy of Thierry Mugler, Paris, p. 93; Munster, Westphalisches Landesmuseum, p. 37; National Army Museum, Camberley, p. 31; New York, Fashion Institute of Technology, p. 211: Historical Society, pp. 28, 162–163; By courtesy of Nicholas Oakwell, London, p. 115, photo Andy Knight; Terry O'Neill/Camera Press, p. 90; Paris, Bibliothèque Nationale, Paris, pp. 38, 94, 95, 105, 144: Bibliothèque des Arts Décoratifs, pp. 99, 101, 151: Musée Carnavalet, p. 146: Musée de l'Homme, p. 114: Musée de la Mode, pp. 155, 172, 166, 167; Irving Penn, Courtesy of *Vogue*, Copyright 1992 by the Condé Nast Publ. Inc., pp. 20–21; G. Pinkhassov/Magnum, p. 120; By courtesy of J. Pinturier, Paris, p. 188–189; Popperfoto, pp. 127, 142; Josephine Powell, Rome, pp. 34, 46; Redferns, pp. 86, 87; Royal Photographic Society, pp. 79, 138–139; By courtesy of Yves Saint-Laurent, Paris, p. 205; David Secombe, pp. 214–215; Seeburger Collection, Paris, pp. 105, 144; David Seidner, New York, pp. 22–23, 173, 192; By courtesy of David Shilling, London, pp. 45, 107, 193; Lennox Smillie/Camera Press, p. 35; By courtesy of Graham Smith, pp. 208–209; David Stoddart/Katz Photos, p. 70–71; By courtesy of Sybilla, Madrid, photos Javier Vallhonrat, pp. 139, 212–213; Sygma, pp. 43, 216; By courtesy of Tête-à-Tête, Paris, p. 197; Times Newspapers, p. 200; By courtesy of Philip Treacy, London, p. 201; Treviso, Museo Civico, p. 56, 57; By courtesy of Patricia Underwood, New York, pp. 141, 194; Vienna, Österreichische Nationalbibliothek, p. 8, 39, 64; By courtesy of Virgin Records, London, p. 176, stylist, Judy Blame; Folkwang Museum, Essen, p. 164; By courtesy of Vivienne Westwood, p. 37; M. Wolgensinger, p. 129; Yale Centre of British Art, p. 136.

INDEX